T0234979

A Conceptual Framework for Personalised Learning

Philipp Melzer

A Conceptual Framework for Personalised Learning

Influence Factors, Design, and Support Potentials

With a foreword by Prof. Mareike Schoop, PhD

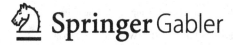 Springer Gabler

Philipp Melzer
Stuttgart, Germany

Dissertation University of Hohenheim, Germany, 2017

D100

Examination Date: December 19th, 2017

Dean: Prof. Dr. Karsten Hadwich
Supervisor: Prof. Mareike Schoop, PhD
Co-Supervisor: Prof. Dr. Georg Herzwurm

ISBN 978-3-658-23094-4   ISBN 978-3-658-23095-1   (eBook)
https://doi.org/10.1007/978-3-658-23095-1

Library of Congress Control Number: 2018950486

Springer Gabler
© Springer Fachmedien Wiesbaden GmbH, part of Springer Nature 2019

This Springer Gabler imprint is published by the registered company Springer Fachmedien
Wiesbaden GmbH part of Springer Nature
The registered company address is: Abraham-Lincoln-Str. 46, 65189 Wiesbaden, Germany

Foreword

Learning is an essential activity in humans. Every information leads to knowledge acquisition based on a learning process. Institutions such as schools and universities need to create learning processes in a way for learnings to achieve the highest possible learning success. This is a challenging goal as lecturers have individual didactic styles and teaching methods and are faced with a plethora of students' learning styles. Up to now it is not possible to address students in large lectures in an individual way most fitting to their personal learning goals, styles, and requirements.

Digitalisation has also affected teaching. Electronic learning is normally used in most universities, but the usage is mostly that of document management. Integrating presence learning and e-learning seems to be a promising approach and is known as "blended learning". The problem of missing personalisation in presence teaching can be solved through an adequate electronic type of teaching with the learners being responsible for their personalisation. However, a mere combination is not enough. An integration of presence learning, and e-learning must be designed in such a way as to combine the advantages of both.

This is the goal of the present work which integrates various approaches from learning sciences and information systems and applying them to electronic negotiations. As one of the very few approaches, the current work covers the complete design cycle of self-regulated personalised blended learning from its conceptualisation to its implementation and finally its evaluation, also assessing influence factors for optimal learning success.

The present work has important contributions for research as well as for practice. Researchers in information systems will find a novel approach to self-regulation and personalisation in the integration of e-learning and presence learning. Researchers in learning science will find the PLF deeply rooted in theory and useful as a basis for designing blended learning approaches. Teachers will find a complete example of a blended learning approach including the very rare extensive evaluation of such approach.

All in all, the book provides excellent research and deserves widespread dissemination.

Professor Mareike Schoop, PhD

Preface

This thesis' origin can be best described by the following quote from John Dewey:

"Cease conceiving of education as mere preparation for later life, and make it the full meaning of the present life." (Dewey 1893, p. 660)

Besides a large interest in learning about a broad range of different topics, I always enjoyed observing and controlling my own learning behaviour with the goal of learning more effectively and efficiently. Having sparked my interest during schooling and academic studies, I got the opportunity to investigate learning processes within this PhD thesis and at the same time making learning the full meaning of my life as a researcher.

In the beginning this was not an easy endeavour since, having a degree in information systems, I lacked the theoretical foundations from the learning sciences as well as experience in designing learning interventions, which had to be developed first. Furthermore, this thesis fell in turbulent times seeing a transformation of traditional education by digital processes, applications, and tools making necessary a thorough investigation of socio-technical aspects in digital education from the perspective of information systems. In particular, this thesis investigates the personalisation of learning as a means to address the diversity and heterogeneity of learners in lifelong formal and informal learning scenarios.

Beginning with an analysis of the controversial literature on individual learning styles and matching teaching methods, this thesis argues for a broader foundation of personalised learning creating the personalised learning framework. Based on this framework, a flipped classroom course design is developed, implemented, and evaluated at the University of Hohenheim. However, this thesis represents only a first step into digitising education, unravelling new potentials and challenges for further investigation such as automated adaptive personalised learning, digital collaborative learning, or learning analytics. This thesis targets researchers from the domains of information systems and the learning sciences as well as practitioners in learning and teaching, designers of learning tools, educational institutions, and policy makers.

Completing a PhD thesis would not be possible without the support of many people. Thus, I want to thank everybody who supported me during my PhD project. Especially, I want to thank my supervisor Prof. Mareike

Schoop, PhD, co-supervisor Prof. Dr. Georg Herzwurm, and Prof. Dr. Katja Schimmelpfeng for chairing the board of examiners.

I want to thank my supervisor Prof. Mareike Schoop, PhD for raising my curiosity for research very early and supporting my scientific career from the very beginning. She gave me the opportunity to pursue this new topic in her group and encouraged me numerous times to present and discuss contributions at international conferences. In addition to that, she allowed me to redesign one of her favourite lectures at the same time continuously scrutinising and challenging the ideas of this thesis.

Furthermore, I want to express gratitude to my colleagues at the Information Systems 1 Department Dr. Bernd Schneider, Annika Lenz, Michael Körner, Dr. Alexander Dannenmann, Prof. Dr. Marc Fernandes, Dr. Johannes Gettinger, Simon Bumiller, Andreas Schmid, Muhammed-Fatih Kaya, Corina Blum, and Franziska Joustra for the great working atmosphere, their continuous support, and numerous discussions. I also want to thank Dr. Per van der Wijst from Tilburg University for the fruitful collaboration in several negotiation simulations.

I want to thank my father Wolfgang Melzer for raising me as a single father, his material and immaterial support, and for providing me with the freedom to pursue my goals.

Finally, I extend the greatest gratitude to my fiancée Annika Lenz, who did not only support me as a colleague but also had to compromise a lot during the final months before thesis submission. Her appreciation and tireless support far beyond comprehension gave me the power to succeed. I love you!

Stuttgart-Hohenheim, Mai 2018
Philipp Melzer

Table of Contents

List of Figures

List of Tables

List of Abbreviations

ACM	Association for Computer Machinery
ANOVA	Analysis of Variance
ANM	Advanced Negotiation Management
AVE	Average Variance Extracted
CPR	Computers and People Research
COI	Community of inquiry
DBR	Design-Based Research
ECIS	European Conference for Information Systems
EUT	End-User Training
ICIS	International Conference for Information Systems
ILIAS	Integriertes Lern-, Informations- und Arbeitskooperations-System (German for Integrated Learning, Information, and Work Cooperation System)
IS	Information System
ISSM	Information Systems Success Model
KMO	Kaiser-Mayer-Olkin
LSQ	Learning Styles Questionnaire
M	Mean
Mdn	Median
MSLQ	Motivated Strategies for Learning Questionnaire
NEGOXP	Face-To-Face Negotiation Experience
NMC	New Media Consortium
NSS	Negotiation Support System
NSSXP	Electronic Negotiation Experience
PLE	Personalised Learning Environment
PLF	Personalised Learning Framework

SCT	Social Cognitive Theory
SIGMIS	Special Interest Group Management Information Systems
SVO	Social Value Orientation
SD	Standard Deviation
TAM	Technology Acceptance Model
UKAIS	UK Academy for Information Systems
VLE	Virtual Learning Environment

1 Towards a Design-Oriented Approach for the Investigation of Self-Regulated Personalised Blended Learning

In a world of increasing complexity driven by the megatrends of globalisation and digitalisation, proper education is becoming increasingly important. Requirements regarding knowledge, skills, and abilities for individuals are constantly rising with the advancing integration and standardisation of markets, transportation, and communication infrastructure reinforced by digital technologies. While education in previous decades was largely bound to formal face-to-face learning in schools, higher education institutions, or professional trainings, the advent of the worldwide web as the global infrastructure for knowledge exchange and collaboration led to disruptive changes redefining education and learning (Tapscott and Williams 2010): (1) Learning is informal as it is performed more often at home or at the workplace in a self-regulated manner, addressing the notion of life-long learning in keeping up with a steadily growing body of knowledge (Marsick and Watkins 2001); (2) Learning is supported by electronic means which quickly developed from a mere substitute of traditional learning to augmenting, modifying, and even redefining learning (Puentedura 2003); (3) Learning is ubiquitous and even electronic support only requires access to the Internet, which is accessible to more and more people from all around the globe in a broad range of situations (Heggestuen 2013); (4) Learning is social with social media encouraging Internet users in the co-creation and exchange of knowledge leading to the formation of online communities and collaborative learning in electronic environments (Brown and Adler 2008).

1.1 Equal Progressions in Pedagogy and Technology

Combining these developments, electronic learning promises benefits such as cost efficiency, availability, flexibility, repeatability, convenience, and consistency (Acton et al. 2005; Gunasekaran et al. 2002), while also showing disadvantages such as missing social context, delayed feedback, or unclear learning objectives (Renner et al. 2015). Blended learning, which is defined as the meaningful integration of face-to-face and online learning (Garrison and Vaughan 2011), aims to provide the best of both worlds. In scenarios where face-to-face meetings as well as online learning are possible (such as in traditional higher education), blended learning has

© Springer Fachmedien Wiesbaden GmbH, part of Springer Nature 2019
P. Melzer, *A Conceptual Framework for Personalised Learning*,
https://doi.org/10.1007/978-3-658-23095-1_1

been found to be a very promising approach to teaching and learning (Hill et al. 2016; Garrison and Vaughan 2011). Blended learning, in various forms, is already today's standard form of learning at German universities supporting presence lectures with the online provision of learning materials or communication facilities (Persike and Friedrich 2016). Currently over 500 different Virtual Learning Environments (VLEs) are on the market worldwide, representing a strongly segmented market regarding different industries, educational institutions, regions, and features. Market growth is projected to be up to 23.17% for 2017 and 2018. The most popular VLEs according to their number of customers are Edmodo, Moodle, Blackboard, and Collaborize Classroom (Pappas 2015; Hill 2015). The VLE ILIAS ("Integriertes Lern-, Informations- und Arbeitskooperationssystem" German for Integrated Learning, Information, and Work Cooperation System), which is primarily used in Western Europe and will be used in this thesis, cites installations at 91 higher education institutions worldwide (ILIAS e.V. 2016). Blended learning is, therefore, evaluated as a short-term trend being easily implementable (Johnson et al. 2016).

The described technological progress in learning is complemented by a similar development within pedagogy. In the year 1910, John Dewey (1997, p. 46) noted the core idea of personalised learning for the first time describing the goal of teaching to be

> "concerned with providing conditions so adapted to individual needs and powers as to make for the permanent improvement of observation, suggestion, and investigation."

However, these ideas have been overshadowed by the prominent learning theories of the following decades, namely behaviourism (Skinner 1958) and cognitivism (Tennyson 1992), which focus on learning processes as a transmission of knowledge from teacher to learner. Behaviourism considers the human mind as a black box focusing on input and output of stimuli. The teacher is the dominant actor as she exerts such stimuli to trigger learning processes. Desired learning behaviour must then be reinforced while undesired learning behaviour must be punished to improve learning. Behaviourist learning methods often focus on rote learning. For example, memorising the vocabulary of a language. As a countermovement to behaviourism, cognitivism investigates the interior of the behaviourist black box, aiming to disentangle the process of human understanding. In contrast to behaviourism, learning is now seen as an activity building on cognitive abilities and prior knowledge of the learners. Learning outcomes are influenced by the learner's metacognition and what is learnt (Shuell 1986). However, only the constructivist learning paradigm (Papert 1993; Harel and Papert 1993) takes up Dewey's considerations going even further and changing education drastically by making the learners themselves responsible for their learning. According to constructivism, there is no knowledge transmission from teacher to learner. Instead, the learners explore and construct knowledge themselves based on their experiences. Constructionism, furthermore, emphasises the importance of situated and collaborative learning (Kafai 2006). Communication and discussion between the teacher as a moderator and the learners as well as between learners themselves are key to confirm the constructed knowledge. The remainder of this thesis will adhere to the constructionist paradigm in particular.

Dewey – rediscovered as an early proponent of constructionist ideas (Brown 1992) – emphasised the relevance of individual needs and powers showing that there is no one-size-fits-all-approach to learning. This is reflected in a shift from clearly defined syllabi to competence-based learning (Erpenbeck and Hasebrook 2011), where learners are able to choose what they want to learn in a self-regulated way, thus, reflecting increasing heterogeneity within the learners and their requirements (Tsai et al. 2013). Such heterogeneity can be divided into persistent characteristics (e.g. gender, age), semi-persistent characteristics (e.g. level of competence, personality traits, or learning styles) that may change slowly over time, and volatile characteristics (e.g. emotional states) that influence the learning process (Gupta et al. 2010). Among the aforementioned influence factors, probably the most intensively used measure of personalisation in learning are learning styles. Drawing from psychological types (Jung 1923) and personality traits (e.g. the Myers Briggs Type Indicator; Myers et al. 1985), over 70 different theories of learning styles were published that can be grouped into five families, ranging from constitutionally based theories to volatile learning approaches (Coffield et al. 2004). In conjunction with the notion of personalised learning, these learning style theories are often easy to understand concepts that are used by teachers, policy makers, or managers. From a scientific point of view, they often contradict each other, providing inconclusive evidence (Pashler et al. 2009). In recent years, personalisation was introduced into educational institutions by policy makers or private dedication e.g. in Germany (Bönsch 2016) or the United States of America (Bill and Melinda Gates Foundation 2014; Pane et al. 2015) to provide equal chances for all learners at the same time, increasing learning performance. Combining the pedagogical and technological perspective, personalised learning was recently named as one of the key trends for higher education (Adams Becker et al. 2017; Moore 2016; Johnson et al. 2016; Johnson et al. 2015).

1.1.1   Perspectives on Personalised Learning

Reflecting the aforementioned technological and pedagogical develop-ments e-learning is defined as

> "electronically mediated asynchronous and synchronous communication for the purpose of constructing and confirming knowledge." (Garrison 2011, p. 2)

By adopting this definition, the impact of constructionism is acknowledged as having communication at the heart of learning. Personalised learning, furthermore, consists of differentiation and individualisation (U.S. Depart-ment of Education 2010). Whilst differentiation aims to tailor the method of teaching according to the learners' preferences, individualisation enables learners to progress through the learning material in their own pace, skip-ping or repeating topics if necessary. Learning goals, however, always stay the same. To implement the personalisation of learning two avenues emerged:

Self-regulated learning is usually investigated within academic learn-ing as it requires learners to be metacognitively, motivationally, and behav-iourally active in their own learning including specified learning strategies as well as perceptions of their own self-efficacy (Zimmerman 1989). Self-regulated personalised learning follows the ideas of the constructionist learning paradigm, making the learners themselves responsible for the personalisation. Consequently, the learners decide when, where, and how to tackle exercises being guided by the teacher. Electronic learning and especially blended learning are key methods to support self-regulated per-sonalised learning, providing the necessary availability and flexibility. How-ever, learners have to be encouraged as well as prepared for personalisa-tion, as it requires profound knowledge about their learning preferences (i.e. metacognition) as well as digital literacy.

Adaptive learning aims to track the learning trajectory automatically, evaluating whether and how a learner performs exercises. This information is then used to recommend further tasks, repeating the same knowledge in case the solution is incorrect or expanding to new and more complex exercises and topics. In a nutshell, adaptive learning aims to personalise learning in an automated way relying on software, building e.g. upon the ideas of intelligent tutoring systems (Anderson et al. 1985; Koedinger and Corbett 2006). Such approaches, however, require the mathematical modelling of the knowledge space (Falmagne et al. 2006; Erpenbeck and Sauter 2013) of the topic to be learned as well as learning with exercises which can be evaluated automatically. This could be achieved for mathematical education for example, while less well-structured topics such as politics can hardly be modelled like that. Recent technological innovations in the context of big data and machine learning such as learning analytics (Greller and Drachsler 2012), however, have drastically increased the interest of researchers and practitioners in this topic again, leading to several highly-valued start-ups (Emerson 2013). Whilst both approaches are very promising and might eventually converge, complementing each other (Steiner et al. 2009), this thesis focuses on the self-regulated approach towards personalised learning, empowering the learners to personalise their learning themselves.

Self-regulated personalised blended learning requires careful coordination of didactics, technology, and content. It is facilitated by constructionist learning methods focusing on situatedness, communication, and collaboration. One specific method of implementing blended learning, which particularly facilitates self-regulated personalisation, is the flipped classroom (also known as inverted classroom; EDUCAUSE Learning Initiative 2012; Feldstein and Hill 2016). While traditional teaching (e.g. in lectures) aims to present theoretical knowledge to the learners, which is in turn applied and evaluated in homework and exercises, the flipped classroom turns these phases around. The preparation phase comes first, in which the learners acquire theoretical knowledge using distant learning supported by e-learning approaches. Within this phase, learning is rather teacher-centred, presenting explicit instructions and prescriptions to the learners. The following presence phase focuses on the application and evaluation of the previously acquired knowledge in interactive role-plays, discussions and case studies. The fact that teacher and learners are co-present facilitates interaction and student-centred learning (Bishop and Verleger 2013). Besides its obvious benefits implementing self-regulated personalised blended learning (Bishop and Verleger 2013; Feldstein and

Hill 2016), flipped classrooms are used frequently in higher education and large classes (Pierce and Fox 2012; Milman 2012). Flipped classrooms require a high amount of metacognitive knowledge, self-discipline, and digital literacy of the learners to prepare before the presence lectures, which is mostly present in higher education. There, however, flipped classrooms can be used to educate large amounts of students at the same time, since the usage of electronic learning approaches enables scalable and repeatable learning. Interaction and discussion during the presence phase is guided by the lecturer, which requires profound knowledge, however, in the end discussions should be encouraged within the group of learners. Finally, the flipped classroom especially supports a large variety of learning tasks used at the same time focusing on active and collaborative learning especially suitable for learning practical procedures (Pierce and Fox 2012; Milman 2012). Literature on the design and evaluation of blended learning courses – especially flipped classrooms – remains scarce (Abeysekera and Dawson 2014; McNally et al. 2017). Apart from theoretical descriptions of underlying learning paradigms and methods, concrete teaching cases and instantiations are rarely published. Such instantiations, however, are important for practitioners who need to apply the theoretical concepts to concrete topics, lectures, and institutions. According to Findlay-Thompson and Mombourquette (2014) even for the flipped classroom there is no one-size-fits-all approach and e.g. the weight of the preparation phase and presence phase has to be adjusted carefully. Also, from a scientific point of view, evaluation methods of such flipped classroom approaches require further research, as instruments often focus solely on the presence or online phases, neglecting their integration (Bishop and Verleger 2013).

1.1.2   Research Questions and Scope

The overall research goal of this thesis is to improve learning by facilitating self-regulated personalisation. It therefore combines the described streams of self-regulated personalisation of learning with methods of blended learning, which are used to support such personalisation. The thesis therefore investigates two distinct research questions (RQs):

Research question 1: Which factors influence self-regulated personalised learning?

Research Question 2: How can self-regulated personalised learning be implemented in blended learning scenarios?

Research question 1 aims for the description of a holistic framework of self-regulated personalised learning including all relevant influence factors as well as being able to theorise how these factors shape personalised learning. Research question 1 is addressed by Melzer and Schoop (2016; cf. chapter 2), who investigate learning styles and teaching methods as a measure of personalised learning with respect to improving learning outcomes. Melzer and Schoop (2015; cf. chapter 3) theorise on the Personalised Learning Framework (PLF), a conceptual framework for personalised learning using learning tasks as the unit of personalisation dwelling on the results of Melzer and Schoop (2016).

Research question 2 is addressed by Melzer and Schoop (2017a; cf. chapter 4), consequently using the conceptual framework to implement a self-regulated personalised flipped classroom within a real university course environment. This proof-of-concept shows relevant requirements and components of such a course design as well as an evaluation approach, which is described in Melzer and Schoop (2017b; cf. chapter 5). While the transformed course remains bound to its specific topic, design requirements, components, and the approach towards evaluation are generalisable to other domains.

The thesis at hand investigates its research questions within the application domains of (electronic) negotiation teaching in higher education. Higher education, especially at universities, shows the necessity for personalised learning, as large numbers of learners with great heterogeneity have to be taught in an effective, but also scalable and cost-efficient manner. Due to lacking financial support, universities often miss sufficient personnel and time for effective teaching. On the one hand, this inhibits satisfaction of the teaching staff with their work. On the other hand, it harms student success leading to increased drop-out rates and duration of study (Leidenfrost et al. 2009). Learners in higher education match the requirements of self-regulated personalised blended learning, as they are usually experienced learners with several years of previous schooling and digital literacy.

Teaching negotiations is relevant in academic as well as practical contexts and thus, often integrated in business or information systems (IS) curricula in higher education or provided in corporate trainings directed at employees managing procurement or sales processes. Negotiation teaching requires the combination of theoretical knowledge and their application

in practical exercise to create necessary skills (Lewicki 1997). Often re-
nowned negotiation experts are integrated into such trainings to show their
best practices providing the possibility to imitate their behaviour (Loewenstein and Thompson 2006). Nowadays negotiations are often conducted
using electronic media such as email (Schoop et al. 2008). Therefore, it is
necessary to integrate face-to-face negotiations as well as electronic negotiation media into teaching (Köszegi and Kersten 2003). However, negotiations as a soft-skill topic usually follows intrinsic motivation to learn
about it and, therefore, create large involvement with the learners (Lewicki
1997). While Melzer and Schoop (2016) analyse end-user-trainings
(EUTs), where future users of the negotiation support system (NSS) Negoisst (Schoop 2010) are trained how to use it correctly to achieve their
goals as part of a university lecture, Melzer and Schoop (2017a) transform
and evaluate the complete university course Advanced Negotiation Management (ANM) into a self-regulated personalised flipped classroom.

1.2   A Design-Oriented Research Methodology

The present work follows a design-oriented research approach. Both – ISs
and the learning sciences – engaged in design science respectively design-based research (DBR) both following a pragmatist epistemology. The
paradigm of pragmatism incorporates the assumption that all research artefacts must be evaluated by their purpose (Thayer 2012). If an artefact is
used in practice, it has a purpose and therefore provides utility. John
Dewey (2013) describes the method of controlled inquiry as a method for
common learning and scientific investigation to uncover new generalisable
truths. It encompasses two phases:

1) the conceptual development of artefacts and
2) their application in practice.

The application of new artefacts to practice is understood as a social action, which leads to modifications of the real world affecting people and
organisations (Mead 1913). Thus, the researcher is often directly involved
into pragmatist research. These fundamental assumptions – reflecting the
practical and social nature of the much later developed learning paradigm
of constructionism – are purported to pragmatist research methodologies
such as design-oriented research, action research, or mixed methods research (Baskerville and Myers 2004; Johnson and Onwuegbuzie 2004).

Design science research as well as DBR are described as methods, which solve problems within their natural environment by designing solutions (Simon 1996). Design-oriented research, therefore, shares its roots with Action Research. However, it does not just focus on the needs of a specific problem but aims for the generalisation of the solution to a class of general problems and theories (Barab and Squire 2004).

1.2.1 Design Science Research in Information Systems

Design science as a research approach in ISs emerged with the seminal article by Hevner et al. (2004) combining earlier streams of research. Figure 1 shows the information systems research framework (Hevner et al. 2004, p. 80) defining ISs research as devoted to rigour and relevance. While scientific rigour is ascertained by embedding research into related theoretical foundations (e.g. theories, frameworks, instruments, etc.) and adhering to scientific methodologies (e.g. data analysis techniques, formalisms, measures, etc.), relevance stems from people, organisations, and technology dealing with the problem in practice. In other words, rigour builds upon the scientific body of knowledge applying it to the research problem, while relevance is grounded into business needs formulated by the environment. IS research aims to develop and justify theories respectively build and evaluate artefacts encompassing instantiations, methods, models, or constructs (Gregor and Hevner 2013) in an iterative way. In the end, ISs research serves a twofold aim as it

1) extends the knowledge base creating new foundations and methodologies and
2) must be applicable to the environment improving practice.

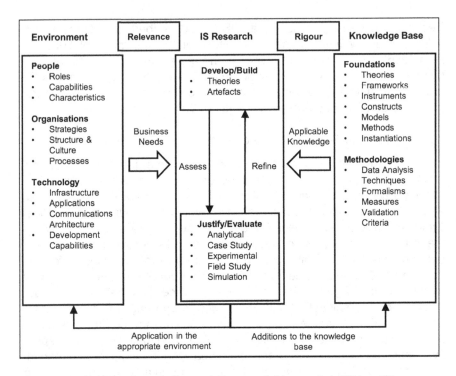

Figure 1   Information Systems Research Framework (Hevner et al. 2004, p. 80)

The ISs research framework allows numerous research methodologies among them behavioural science, focusing on the development and justification of theories, as well as design science, focusing on building and evaluating artefacts. While behavioural science is purported to exhibit high levels of rigour often relying on quantitative methods and statistical analyses, it is criticised because of its lack of relevance being disconnected to practice (Baskerville and Pries-Heje 2010; Hevner et al. 2004). In contrast, design science research aims to provide relevance as well as rigour referring to people, organisations, and technology describing the problem environment as well as foundations and methodologies from the scientific knowledge base. Business needs and scientific knowledge are embodied into the building and evaluation of artefacts, eventually feeding back business applications and additions to the knowledge base. However, design science research is also criticised for low levels of scientific rigour, since many publications focus on instantiations as artefacts analysing software prototypes without abstraction (Gregor and Hevner 2013). However, from its seminal publication in 2004 until today, the applications of design science research have been specified further including detailed methods to clarify the goals of a design science research project (ibid.), structured process models and frameworks to rigorously build (Baskerville and Pries-Heje 2010) and evaluate (Venable et al. 2016) artefacts. Therefore, design science research can be regarded as an acknowledged method of ISs research today.

1.2.2   Design-Based Research in the Learning Sciences

In the learning sciences, a similar stream of research emerged proposing so-called design experiments as a counterpart to behavioural research combining previous approaches to the research methodology of DBR (Collins 1992; Brown 1992). The rediscovery of John Dewey's works on pragmatism (2013) and constructivist thinking (1997) led to a combination of conceptual research and application to the practice of teaching and learning. DBR aims to help learners as well as teachers improving their practices. DBR focuses on six main aspects (Anderson and Shattuck 2012):

1) the design or significant modification of a learning intervention;
2) its implementation within a situated real-life context;
3) its evaluation using mixed methods;
4) continuous improvement of design principles;
5) iterative improvement;
6) joint work between researchers and practitioners.

DBR puts the form of instruction under focus within a realistic context. In contrast to controlled laboratory experiments that are employed in behavioural science, modifications of real learning interventions can be assessed over a long duration (e.g. a whole school year or semester) providing extensive potential for investigation. DBR provides rich insights not only into learning outcomes, but a large plethora of contextual, social, and technological variables including the process of designing and evaluating the learning intervention itself (Barab 2006; Brown 1992). DBR has, therefore, been described to be particularly useful for the investigation of e-learning or blended learning interventions (Wang and Hannafin 2005). However,

DBR faces similar criticism as design science research regarding method-ological rigour, therefore, rigour must be provided by a strong foundation of the problem under investigation within theory and design (Confrey 2006). The learning intervention must be conducted adequately, aiming towards an ethically sound improvement of the identified problem. Further-more, deducted claims must be justifiable with respect to the underlying theory and data as well as relevant and feasible for practitioners. Overall, DBR mostly follows the same assumptions and goals as design science research, applying them to the learning sciences. Compared to design sci-ence research, however, DBR has inspired less publications and therefore received significantly less attention in research and practice (Anderson and Shattuck 2012).

1.3 Synthesis and Resulting Approach

The present thesis combines design science in ISs and DBR in the learning sciences to answer the formulated research questions. Such an approach is necessary for a meaningful evaluation of self-regulated personalisation as it is performed by the learners together with peers and lecturers based on their preferences, experience, and context. Such situations can hardly be created in a laboratory experiment, albeit requiring large compromises regarding the richness of the data gathered. Furthermore, the chosen ap-proach emphasises the relevance of the research regarding the improve-ment of higher education using recent learning methods, e-learning tech-nology and the direct connection between higher education and research at universities. Therefore, the research questions are answered sequen-tially.

1) In an explorative stage, personalised learning is assessed con-ducting a laboratory experiment comparing two learning interven-tions – one focusing on self-regulated learning and one focusing on lecturer-centred learning (chapter 2). The study itself comprises of a build and evaluate phase, firstly creating personalised train-ings, secondly evaluating them empirically regarding learning out-comes. Chapter 3 builds upon the results of the previous chapter theorising on the PLF. The result of stage 1 represents the PLF as a conceptual model of self-regulated personalised learning.

2) In a confirmative stage the PLF is evaluated within a realistic en-vironment. Therefore, a university course is transformed into a

self-regulated personalised flipped classroom using the PLF as a basis. An explanatory design theory is developed deriving general requirements regarding such a course from the literature leading to general course components which are eventually implemented (Baskerville and Pries-Heje 2010). The resulting course design (chapter 4) is implemented and evaluated over a complete semester to generate findings about the course itself as well as the underlying framework. Within this evaluation a mixed-methods approach is chosen, combining qualitative observations and interviews complemented with quantitative surveys to achieve a holistic picture, which is described in chapter 5 (Johnson and Onwuegbuzie 2004; Venkatesh et al. 2013). The result of stage 2, therefore, is a generalisable approach for designing and evaluating self-regulated personalised learning courses, which is not only bound to the course transformed within this thesis. While the exploration of the problem domain and the conceptualisation on the PLF provide an artificial and formative evaluation relying on rigour provided by empirical research and literature, the confirmative stage aims for a naturalistic and summative evaluation of the whole concept (Venable et al. 2016).

Gregor and Hevner (2013) present three types of design science contributions from situated implementations of an artefact over nascent design theories to well-developed design theories. While situated implementations focus on specific and limited scenarios providing less mature knowledge, well-developed design theories provide abstract, complete, and mature knowledge about a phenomenon. This thesis aims for a nascent design theory of self-regulated personalised blended learning including operational knowledge on design principles and architectures as well as the situated implementation of the framework itself. The targeted contribution of this work can be categorised according to the dimensions of solution maturity and application domain maturity (Gregor and Hevner 2013). If maturity is high on both dimensions, the contribution lies in the application of known solutions to known problems, which is not a scientific knowledge contribution (cf. Figure 2). If new solutions are developed for known problems, this is categorised as an improvement, whereas the extension of known solutions to new problems is called an exaptation – both presenting valuable research opportunities. Eventually, low solution maturity paired with low application domain maturity leads to an invention combining new solutions and new problems, eventually describing a valuable but complex research opportunity.

Since there is already a large number of publications dealing with the topic of personalising learning the application domain maturity can be considered to be high. The presented solution, using a self-regulated approach in combination with blended learning is rather new, characterising solution maturity to be low. Hence, the present work aims to contribute an improvement to self-regulated personalised learning providing new solutions (i.e. PLF) to the known problem of personalised learning.

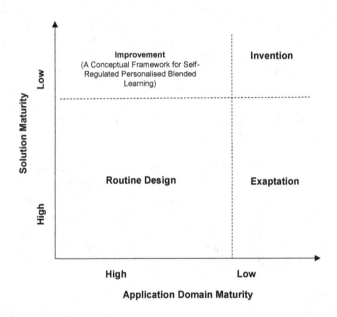

Figure 2   Contributions of Design Science Research (adapted from Gregor and Hevner 2013, p. 345)

The structure of this thesis is outlined in Figure 3. Chapter 1 introduces the topic and describes the selected research methodology following a design-oriented approach. Chapter 2 presents a study on personalised learning investigating the matching of learning styles and teaching methods showing that learning styles are not the only relevant factor for personalised learning. Chapter 3 builds on these findings, presenting a conceptual framework for task and tool personalisation. Based on the theory of cognitive fit, the framework aims to define all relevant factors of personalised learning and their relationships. This framework is consequently implemented in chapters 4 and 5. While chapter 4 describes the design of a university course implementing the PLF, chapter 5 focuses on an evaluation concept aiming to generalise the findings of this work. Chapter 6 discusses findings of the presented studies in a holistic manner, also describing limitations of the chosen approach, concluding this work summarising its contributions and presenting implications for research and practice as well as potential for future research.

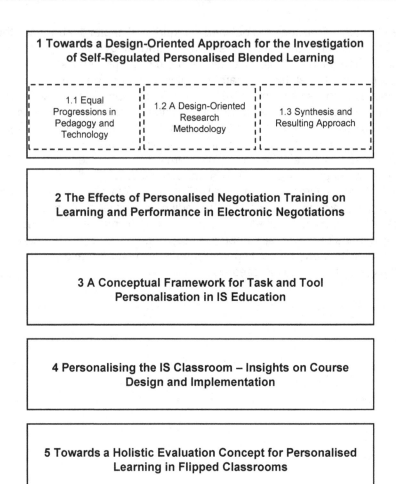

1 Towards a Design-Oriented Approach for the Investigation of Self-Regulated Personalised Blended Learning

| 1.1 Equal Progressions in Pedagogy and Technology | 1.2 A Design-Oriented Research Methodology | 1.3 Synthesis and Resulting Approach |

2 The Effects of Personalised Negotiation Training on Learning and Performance in Electronic Negotiations

3 A Conceptual Framework for Task and Tool Personalisation in IS Education

4 Personalising the IS Classroom – Insights on Course Design and Implementation

5 Towards a Holistic Evaluation Concept for Personalised Learning in Flipped Classrooms

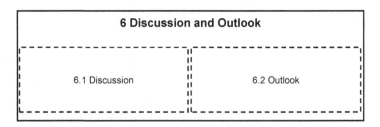

6 Discussion and Outlook

| 6.1 Discussion | 6.2 Outlook |

Figure 3   Structure of the Thesis

2 The Effects of Personalised Negotiation Training on Learning and Performance in Electronic Negotiations

Abstract
Individuals have different learning styles and thus require different methods for knowledge acquisition. Whereas learning theories have long acknowledged this fact, personalised negotiation trainings especially for electronic negotiations have rarely been developed. This paper integrates learning styles and negotiation styles and reports on an implementation of this integration. We will discuss personalised negotiation trainings, namely an enactive training and a vicarious training, that we developed to match the learners' learning styles. Such a matching is proposed to be beneficial regarding learning outcomes. Furthermore, positive effects on the dyadic negotiation outcomes are assumed. To this end, an experiment with participants from different European countries was conducted. The results show tendencies that personalised negotiation trainings lead to better skill acquisition during the training and also to fairer negotiation outcomes. Overall, this paper contributes an integration of the theories on individual differences from the domains of negotiation and learning as well as valuable insights for further experiments on individual differences in negotiations.

Co-Author
Prof. Mareike Schoop, PhD

© Springer Fachmedien Wiesbaden GmbH, part of Springer Nature 2019
P. Melzer, *A Conceptual Framework for Personalised Learning*,
https://doi.org/10.1007/978-3-658-23095-1_2

2.1 Personalised Negotiation Training to Improve Electronic Negotiation Skills

Negotiations within or between companies are daily business tasks for managers who are expected and required to be skilled negotiators achieving optimal negotiation outcomes, saving costs, and establishing long lasting relationships with important business partners. Negotiators, therefore, need to acquire years of experience and/or attend proper training. Such experience or training is very expensive; thus, skilled negotiators are often considered to be valuable company assets. In management education, the topic of negotiation training emerged in the 1980s and provoked much research until today. Research on electronic NSSs shows the willingness of negotiators to use such systems simulating negotiations to try out different strategies (Vetschera et al. 2006). Since the development of the first NSS, more and more support functionalities have been integrated to provide holistic support (Schoop 2010). At the same time, context-sensitive NSSs have been called for which present only relevant information and support features to the negotiators, based on their individual characteristics (Gettinger et al. 2012).

End-user training (EUT) has been found to increase utility and adoption of ISs (Igbaria et al. 1995). EUTs have also been the focus of research on the integration and evaluation of individual characteristics of learners and training methods providing a personalised approach (Gupta and Anson 2014). However, current trainings in companies still follow the same teaching (and thus learning) approach for all participants.

Bringing together the needs for negotiation training in companies and personalised EUTs, our research aim is to develop a framework for personalised e-negotiation trainings. Those trainings are evaluated pursuing the research question whether negotiators attending personalised trainings with training methods matching their personal learning styles achieve better learning and negotiation outcomes than those with a mismatch between learning style and training method. The outcomes are tested in the EUT as well as in a subsequent negotiation experiment using an NSS.

To this end, the methodology of DBR is used (Brown 1992). DBR focuses on the development, evaluation, and iterative improvement of learning interventions within real-life educational scenarios aiming at enhancing design principles and at deriving new theories.

2.2 Creating Personalised Negotiation Trainings Based on End-User Training Best Practices

The EUT framework structures the complete process of preparing, conducting and evaluating an EUT beginning with the pre-training phase, describing the actual learning process influenced by the training method used, eventually leading to specific learning outcomes (cf. Figure 4).

Most importantly, EUTs have to be adapted to the specific target system; in our case the NSS Negoisst (Schoop et al. 2003; Schoop 2010). In the pre-training phase, training goals have to be defined which relate to the learning outcomes to be measured afterwards. These learning outcomes can be differentiated into skills, cognitive outcomes, affective outcomes, and metacognitive outcomes following the epistemological perspectives of the designer (Bloom et al. 1984). The current study focuses on the evaluation of learning outcomes especially skills measured directly after the training as well as after the negotiation. The main EUT contains the training method to be implemented, the learning process as well as their interaction. Concerning the method of training, it should be specified whether to use computers as trainers or as a medium of training. The learning techniques also need to be specified. Individual differences of learners influence the learning process, since they need to be supported regarding content as well as process. Learning process and training method will be described in detail in sections 2.2.1 and 2.2.2 as they are vital for the matching of training method and learning style which constitutes the notion of personalised learning used throughout this paper.

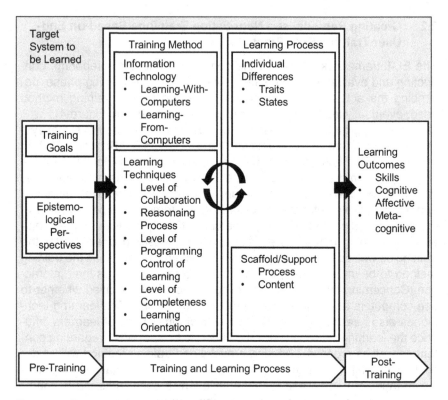

Figure 4   Framework for End-User Training Research (adapted from Gupta and Bostrom 2006, p. 173; Gupta et al. 2010, p.12)

2.2.1   Training Methods and Related Learning Techniques

Recent studies on EUT research concentrate on social cognitive theory (SCT; Gupta et al. 2010). SCT is rooted in the paradigm of constructivism, which is also a prominent approach in e-learning, rejecting traditional knowledge transfer between teachers; instead focusing on the students constructing their knowledge themselves (Kafai 2006).

SCT views learning as the intentional task using direct personal reflection, reflection by others, or interdependent and coordinative learning in groups. SCT distinguishes enactive learning (i.e. observing one's own learning process while constructively acquiring new knowledge) and vicarious learning (i.e. observing and imitating experts to acquire new knowledge). According to SCT, a mix of both methods is the best training method for complex tasks as each method has particular advantages and disadvantages (Gupta et al. 2010).

2.2.2   Learning Process and Individual Differences

For management studies assessing the relationship between tasks and learning preferences, Kolbs' Learning Style Instrument (Kolb 1984) and Honey and Mumford's Learning Style Questionnaire (LSQ; Honey and Mumford 2000) are the most widely used instruments. Both are based on the constructivist model of experiential learning defining learning as a

> "process whereby knowledge is created through the transformation of experi-
> ence" (Kolb 1984, p.41).

Experiential learning is described as a cyclic process following four phases, namely

1)   having a new experience;
2)   reviewing on this experience;
3)   concluding from this experience; and
4)   planning the next steps.

Although learners have to complete all phases they possess individual preferences and skills for one or more of these phases. Accordingly, they can be classified as having activist, reflector, theorist, or pragmatist learning styles (cf. Figure 5). However, these styles are not static but might change depending on the learning task or previous learning experience (Kolb 2000). Learning styles are related to certain behavioural patterns (Honey and Mumford 2000). Activists are described as being open-minded, eager for being exposed to new situations, thus likely to welcome change. They often rush into action without preparation being bored by consolidation tasks. Pragmatists are technology-oriented and eager to test out things in practice. In general, they are more task-oriented than people-oriented. They try to seize the first solution that comes up and reject anything without an obvious application. Overall, activists and pragmatists share numerous properties and are consequently considered as following a practical learning style in the remaining paper.

Reflectors are thorough, methodical thinkers and listeners to assimilate information. They rarely jump to conclusions and, therefore, are rather slow to make up their minds having a tendency to hold back from participation avoiding risks. This leads to a rather unassertive communication style. Theorists represent even more logical and rational thinkers, are often restricted to their thoughts, and have a low tolerance for uncertainty and subjective intuition, aiming to generate sound theories. Reflectors and theorists rely on similar mind-sets and are thus considered to be following a theoretical learning style in our work.

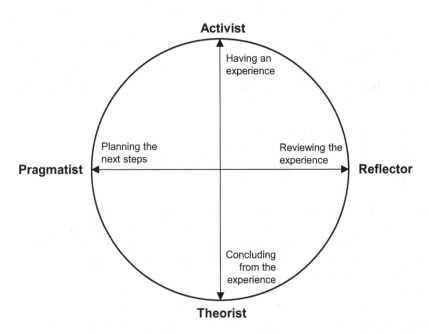

Figure 5   Model of Experiential Learning and Corresponding Learning Styles (adapted from Mumford and Honey 1992, p.10)

2.2.3   Development of Personalised Negotiation Trainings Matching Training Methods and Learning Styles

While negotiation styles are used to identify negotiators and predict their behaviour (de Moura and Seixas Costa 2014) approaches to use individual differences of negotiators to improve learning are not existent to our knowledge. Previous research on EUTs analyses training methods and learning styles and often suggests their interrelation (Sein and Bostrom 1989; Davis and Bostrom 1993). Most studies argue that specific matching combinations between training methods and learning styles are particularly effective. Enactive training methods (emphasising exploration, collaboration, and situatedness) are proposed for practical learning styles whereas vicarious training methods (emphasising reflection, individual learning, and abstract generalisation) are proposed for theoretical learning. Such matching has been demonstrated to induce differences regarding learning outcomes between matches and non-matches (Sein and Bostrom 1989; Bostrom et al. 1990; Gupta and Anson 2014; different opinion is presented by Ruble and Stout 1993).

Integrating the specific requirements of negotiation trainings and EUTs, we developed two EUTs for the NSS Negoisst, namely one for practical and one for theoretical learning styles implemented as an enactive and vicarious training respectively but with identical content (Melzer and Schoop 2014a; Melzer and Schoop 2014b). In the enactive EUT the learners have to acquire negotiation basics, prepare a negotiation, get familiar with Negoisst, and use it to implement their prepared negotiation strategy in a training negotiation, following an inductive trial-and-error approach. The learners explore the tasks collaboratively in groups and later discuss their results in class. The trainer only moderates this discussion and reviews or supplements its results if necessary. Therefore, the learners are in control and a high level of interaction is supported. In the vicarious training, learners are encouraged to learn individually from the trainer as the negotiation expert who always remains in front of the class and presents the contents without much interaction. The trainer presents negotiation preparation basics, strategies as well as the underlying concepts and features of Negoisst in a deductive manner. The learners are then guided through the system by the trainer simulating a ready-made negotiation. Therefore, the vicarious training follows a programmed approach, keeping the trainer in control of the learning.

2.3 Hypotheses

Following DBR, we will derive hypotheses to answer the research question, whether an EUT with matching training method and learning style is superior to non-matching combinations regarding learning as well as negotiation outcomes both on individual and dyad level.

2.3.1   Individual Hypotheses

Typically, objective negotiation performance is evaluated using measures of utility commonly calculated using linear additive preference models showing the achievement of objectives (Keeney and Raiffa 1976). Individual differences in negotiations can be distinguished using the theory of social value orientation (SVO; Messick and McClintock 1968; De Dreu and Boles 1998) or the theory of the managerial grid (Blake and Mouton 1964). While the SVO distinguishes proself negotiators maximising their own gains from prosocial negotiators who are much concerned with others' gains, the managerial grid adds the dimension of assertiveness to the dimension of cooperativeness. The Thomas-Kilmann Conflict MODE instrument (Kilmann and Thomas 1992) defines the negotiation styles accommodating, avoiding, compromising, competing, and collaborating according to their degree of assertiveness or cooperativeness displayed in Figure 6. Based on the description of matching and non-matching combinations in sections 2.2.1 and 2.2.2, negotiation outcomes should be predictable: Practical/enactive negotiators (practical negotiators in the remaining paper) are assumed to be collaborative because of their high social competence working with others and their assertive character. Following this style of negotiation, they should achieve higher individual utilities than other negotiators (Ma et al. 2012). Theoretical/vicarious negotiators (theoretical negotiators in the remaining paper) are assumed to have an avoiding negotiation style, carefully preparing their negotiation strategy and rationally evaluating their next steps, disregarding relationship-building due to low social competence which may set back their negotiation success. Low uncertainty tolerance might lead to suboptimal decisions under uncertainty resulting in lower individual utilities. To predict negotiation behaviour for non-matching negotiators, it is important to know whether the effect of learning styles or training methods is more influential. Assuming both effects being equally important such negotiators avoid extreme behaviour leading to a compromising negotiation strategy. According to previous studies on individual differences (Ma et al. 2012; Gupta and Anson 2014), we assume no effect of a matching on individual utility because the effects

of practical negotiators achieving higher individual utilities, theoretical negotiators achieving lower individual utilities and non-matching negotiators
achieving mediocre individual utilities are balanced out.

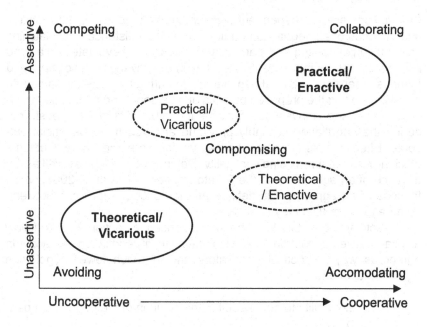

Figure 6   Predicted Negotiation Styles of Matches and Non-Matches Based on the Managerial Grid (Blake and Mouton 1964; Kilmann and Thomas 1992)

Thus, we formulate our individual hypotheses on learning outcomes measured by skill acquisition. To account for electronic negotiations, skill acquisition is distinguished into face-to-face negotiation skill acquisition (H1a)
and electronic negotiation skill acquisition (H1b). Early studies on personalised EUTs could demonstrate improved skill acquisition (Sein and
Bostrom 1989; Bostrom et al. 1990). Thus, we hypothesise, that a matching training method and learning style should lead to better skill acquisition.

H1a: Matching negotiation trainings lead to better perceived acqui-
            sition of face-to-face negotiation skills.

H1b: Matching negotiation trainings lead to better perceived acqui-
            sition of electronic negotiation skills.

2.3.2   Dyadic Hypotheses

Negotiations are interdependent tasks integrating individual skills, styles, and attitudes of all negotiation parties. Thus, the existence of a matching combination of training and learning style needs to be evaluated on a dyad level to assess its influence on negotiation effectiveness, efficiency, and fairness. Therefore, bilateral negotiations featuring two, one, or no negotiator(s) exhibiting the proposed benefits of a personalised negotiation training are analysed to investigate whether those benefits can be transferred during the negotiation probably providing an even more beneficial outcome. Effectiveness is operationalised via the agreement rate. Outcome efficiency is measured using joint utility (Delaney et al. 1997) as well as the distance of an agreement to the Pareto-frontier (Raiffa et al. 2002), while fairness of an agreement is defined as the contract imbalance between both negotiators (Delaney et al. 1997).

Practical negotiators have been categorised in section 2.3.1 to follow a collaborative negotiation style. This affects their negotiation behaviour in numerous ways: Practical negotiators should reach fewer negotiation agreements due to

1) a weak ability to put oneself in the position of the negotiation partner and
2) misconceptions about negotiation goals because of missing preparation.

Furthermore, rushing into a negotiation posing high demands often increases the conflict situation of a negotiation leading to distributive bargaining and a high possibility of impasse situations. Practical negotiators are fast in exchanging offers which should lead to more competitive communication behaviour reducing negotiation effectiveness (Pesendorfer and Köszegi 2006). Regarding negotiation efficiency and fairness, a long period of haggling with only small improvements is often necessary to optimise an agreement. Thus, practical negotiators often fail to achieve efficient and fair outcomes seizing on the first expedient agreement. Theoretical negotiators have a high endurance in optimisation of the agreement and can use the advantages of asynchronous message exchange in negotiations. However, they are restricted to their way of thinking having problems to work with others who rely on a communicative approach or on finding creative solutions. Thus, inconclusive endings of negotiations are also possible. Such behaviour, in line with the notion of the negotiation dilemma, leads to efficient and fair outcomes, but low agreement rates.

Analysing negotiation dyads having the same or different level of cooperativeness has been performed using the SVO (Olekalns and Smith 1999). This study demonstrated that prosocial (corresponding to practical negotiators) dyads explicitly focus on strategies of relationship-building such as supporting the negotiation partner or restructuring the negotiation agenda in potential impasse situations. Proself (corresponding to theoretical negotiators) dyads employ a mixture of relationship-oriented strategies and more task-oriented strategies, e.g. exchanging priority information or making concessions, while mixed dyads solely concentrate on task-focused strategies. It also confirms our notion of a more relationship-oriented focus for equally matching dyads compared to a more task-oriented focus for mixed ones. Thus, we expect more effective and efficient outcomes with fairer agreements for dyads in which the negotiators have the same training method and/or learning style.

H2:   Dyads in which both negotiators attended a matching training achieve more effective outcomes than dyads with only one or no negotiator attending such training.

H3:   Dyads in which both negotiators attended a matching training achieve more efficient outcomes regarding

H3a: joint utility than dyads with only one or no negotiator attending such training.

H3b: distance to the Pareto-frontier than dyads with only one or no negotiator attending such training.

H4:   Dyads in which both negotiators attended a matching training achieve fairer outcomes than dyads with only one or no negotiator attending such training.

2.4   Methodology

To answer the hypotheses, we performed a negotiation experiment which will be described in the following chapter.

2.4.1   Participants

The evaluation of personalised negotiation trainings was conducted involving 178 graduate students from two European universities. 91 students enrolled in communication sciences, 23 in ISs, 22 in management, 16 in international business and economics, 1 in economics, 1 in agribusiness, 20 exchange students, and 4 students of unknown course. All participants attended a one semester course on negotiations and were rewarded for participation in the experiment by receiving credit points.

2.4.2   Experiment Procedure and Measurement

Before the trainings, participants filled in a survey assessing demographics as well as the LSQ to determine their individual learning style (Honey and Mumford 1992). Each participant was then assigned to one of the trainings to create two groups equal in size, previous skills, and distribution of learning styles. After the trainings, a ten-day negotiation simulation with the Negoisst system was conducted to measure task performance, namely negotiation effectiveness, as well as efficiency and fairness of the agreements. Participants negotiated a bilateral buyer-seller dispute resolution scenario. The case includes several distributive and integrative issues to be negotiated focusing on warranty issues of a recently bought laptop. Negotiators were provided issues and preferences per party assuming no alternatives to negotiation. After the negotiation, another survey assessed the acquisition of negotiation and e-negotiation skills.

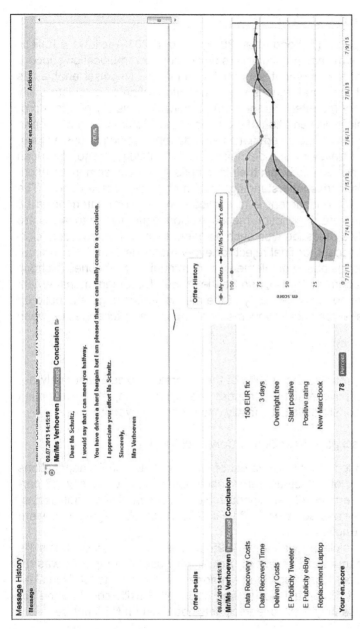

Figure 7   Main Screen of Negoisst

2.4.3   Negoisst System

The NSS Negoisst (Schoop et al. 2003; Schoop 2010) follows a holistic support paradigm implementing decision support, communication support, and document management support (cf. Figure 7). Negoisst enables its users to elicit their preferences using this information to calculate utility values for every (counter)offer sent and received. A history of offers provides a graphic representation of the negotiation. Communication support is realised implementing a negotiation agenda representing issues, values, units, and their relationships defined using an ontology. Negotiators can directly reference issues within their text messages using semantic enrichment. Therefore, misunderstandings and ambiguities are reduced. The aim of pragmatic enrichment is to explicate the sender's intention to be transferred with the negotiation message. Consequently, negotiators are able to specify a message type such as offer, counteroffer, question, clarification, final accept, or final reject for every message sent. The communication support is based on elements of communication theories (Schoop 2005) e.g.: Habermas (1984), and Searle (1969). Document management is implemented to increase clarity of the message exchange and build up trust. Negoisst automatically documents all messages exchanged between negotiators.

2.5   Results

This chapter presents the results of the laboratory experiment firstly describing descriptive results to assess the participants, then presenting measures of construct validity, finally answering the hypotheses.

2.5.1   Descriptive Results and Construct Validity

Data cleaning led to a final data set of 110 negotiators in 55 negotiations each consisting of one student from each participating university. 67 participants were female, 42 participants male with one participant not disclosing gender; average age was 24.8 years (SD=1.92). All negotiations were conducted in English.

Computer skills (Igbaria et al. 1995) and (electronic) negotiation skills of the participants were assessed. Actual daily use of computers was reported to be very high. Participants reported well-above negotiation skills (M=4.69, SD=1.13) on a 7-point Likert scale. NSS skills could not be assessed because only 9.1% of participants had used an NSS before.

The assessment of learning styles led to the treatment groups shown in Table 1.

Table 1   Treatment Groups (Matching Combinations Bold)

Treatments	Enactive Training	Vicarious Training	Total
Activists	**11**	9	20
Pragmatists	**15**	13	28
Reflectors	20	**20**	40
Theorists	11	**11**	22
Total	57	53	110

Manipulation checks showed that both EUTs were perceived significantly different regarding the training methods employed (t(108)=0.639, p<0.001).

Examining task performance of the negotiations, 45 (81,8%) negotiations led to an agreement. Negotiators reaching an agreement achieved individual utilities from 41% to 69% (M=54.52%, SD=6.32). Joint utilities reached from 100% to the Pareto-optimal outcome of 115% (M=109.04%, SD=3.8). Resulting in outcomes directly on the Pareto-frontier to agreements having 7.62 percentage points distance to the Pareto-frontier (M=3.53%, SD=2.9). Fairness of the agreements ranged from perfectly fair agreements to a contract imbalance of 28 percentage points (M=8.96%, SD=8.1).

Appendix A (cf. Table 15) shows the newly developed items for the measurement of the latent individual variables face-to-face (NEGOXP) and e-negotiation skill acquisition (NSSXP). Both constructs were measured using a 7-point Likert scale. An exploratory factor analysis has been performed using principal axis factoring to calculate construct values for the subjective dimensions of interest as they are newly developed. Overall, ten items representing face-to-face negotiation skill acquisition, and electronic negotiation skill acquisition are integrated leading to a Kaiser-Meyer-Olkin-criteria (KMO) of 0.831 showing mediocre relationships in the data set. Two items (NSSXP_3, NEGOXP_4R) had to be excluded during data cleaning. Extraction is performed following Kaiser's criterion to extract all

factors with eigenvalues greater than one leading to two factors representing the theoretical considerations explaining 48.66% of variance (cf. Table
2). Because the constructs used are tightly coupled Oblimin-rotation has
been used (Hair et al. 2010).

Table 2   Factor Loadings After Rotation

	Factor	
	1	2
NSSXP_6	.762	-.013
NSSXP_1	.690	.019
NSSXP_4R	.686	.083
NSSXP_2R	.652	-.053
NSSXP_5 (excluded)	.428	-.284
NEGOXP_1	-.028	-.832
NEGOXP_3	-.095	-.740
NEGOXP_5	.113	-.628
NEGOXP_2R (excluded)	.308	-.414
NEGOXP_6 (excluded)	.385	-.403
KMO Measure of Sampling Adequacy	0.831	
Bartlett's Test of Sphericity	$\chi^2=430.794$***	
Within this thesis the following probability values are applied, unless indicated otherwise: *p<0.05, **p<0.01, ***p<0.001		

To evaluate the validity of the multi-item measurement model, we follow
the guidelines by Hair et al. (2014). To evaluate discriminant validity, cross
loadings and correlations between the factors are assessed. Table 2
shows cross loadings above the 0.200 level for NSSXP_5 as well as NE-
GOXP_2R and NEGOXP_6. Thus, these items are excluded from further
analyses. There is a significant correlation (cf. Table 3) between both factors, representing their theoretical underpinnings as face-to-face negotiation skills are usually a necessary prerequisite to e-negotiation skills
(Köszegi and Kersten 2003).

       Regarding internal consistency reliability, Cronbach's Alpha and com-
posite reliability show values well above the thresholds of 0.5 (Cronbach
1951) and 0.7 respectively (Nunnally and Bernstein 1994) (cf. Table 3).

Indicator reliability requires factor loadings over 0.400 which are matched by all factors.

Analysing convergent validity, the average variance extracted (AVE) is calculated. AVE is typically assumed to be sufficient if greater than 0.5, meaning that a construct explains more than half of the variance of its indicators. Values are rather low for both constructs assessed leaving e-negotiation skill acquisition below the threshold. Further analyses, therefore, have to be performed with caution.

Table 3   Reliability Measures of Measurement Model Including Transformed R-Matrix

	NEGOXP	NSSXP
Arithmetic Mean	5.18	5.8
Cronbach's Alpha	.759	.783
Composite Reliability	.782	.765
Average Variance Extracted	.525	.473
NEGOXP	1	.624**
NSSXP	.624**	1

2.5.2   Hypotheses Testing

Based on the data described in the previous section, we analyse the hypotheses postulated in section 2.3. Following the explanations before, we assign a dichotomous variable to each participant indicating whether training method and learning style are matching or not. Thus, testing the hypotheses demands comparisons between matching and non-matching groups w.r.t. the dependent variables. Data exploration showed that none of these constructs is normally distributed, thus we apply Mann-Whitney tests to compare the treatment groups leading to the results in Table 4. All p-values provided are 2-tailed.

Table 4   Results of Mann-Whitney Tests Comparing Matching and Non-Matching Conditions

		H1a	H1b
	Individual Outcome	NEGOXP	NSSXP
Median Matching (N=57)	55.0%	5.33	6.00
Median Non-Matching (N=53)	52.5%	5.00	5.75
U	992.50	1288.00	1132.50
Significance level	p=0.876	p=0.185	p=0.023
Effect Size	r=0.015	r=0.127	r=0.216*

These tests show a non-significant increase in individual utility and face-to-face negotiation skill acquisition between non-matches and matches. While we expected no effect regarding individual outcomes, we have to reject hypotheses 1a since a matching training method and learning style did not increase face-to-face negotiation skill acquisition significantly. However, the data shows that negotiators with matching training method and learning style have a significantly higher e-negotiation skill acquisition than negotiators without such matching representing a small effect. Thus, we can support hypothesis 1b. However, the analysis of construct validity above led to concerns evaluating electronic negotiation skills because of very low convergent validity.

For further evaluations of the effects of training method and learning style, the two independent variables underlying the matching, training method, and learning style are analysed. Thus, a two-way independent analysis of variance (ANOVA) is conducted to assess main and interaction effects indicating a relationship between the training method and e-negotiation skill acquisition. However, no significant main effects of learning style, training method, or interaction effects are found including covariates such as gender, age, native language, university, or previous computer usage. To evaluate our hypotheses, contrasts were defined to compare practical to theoretical learning styles and activists to pragmatists respectively reflectors to theorists also showing no significant differences. Regarding the effect sizes, training method and learning style have an equally small effect on e-negotiation skill acquisition. Effect sizes get to almost zero analysing the effect on individual utility.

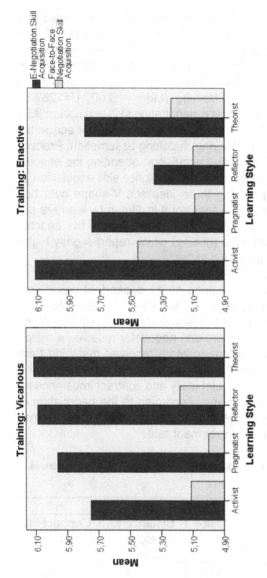

Figure 8   Skill Acquisition for Learners with Enactive and Vicarious Training

Although ANOVA is a rather robust method to deal with non-normally distributed variables, e-negotiation skill acquisition has been analysed further applying a Mann-Whitney test to assess the assumed differences between both training methods precisely. Negotiators attending the vicarious training achieve higher e-negotiation skill acquisition (Mdn = 6.00) compared to negotiators attending the enactive training (Mdn = 6.00, U=1267.50, p=0.147, r=0.139). Figure 8 shows that e-negotiation skill acquisition (Mdn = 6.00) in general was higher than face-to-face negotiation skill acquisition (Mdn = 5.33) and confirms our underlying matching assumption. Practical learning styles mostly report higher skill acquisition attending the enactive training, while theoretical learning styles report higher skill acquisition attending the vicarious training leading to an idealistic V-shape over both diagrams in Figure 8. The assumed linear trend is diluted by learners preferring the opposite style in both briefings (i.e. theorists in the enactive training and activists in the vicarious training) which report slightly higher skill acquisition than their neighbouring styles.

Proceeding to hypotheses 2 - 4, dyadic variables are analysed. An explorative investigation reveals that none of the dependent variables is normally distributed. Thus, non-parametric tests are applied. We distinguish between dyads where none of the negotiators received a matching negotiation training, mixed dyads where one negotiator received a matching training, and dyads where both negotiators received matching trainings. Table 5 shows median values for our measurement variables demonstrating slightly improving effects for joint utility and contract imbalance the more matching negotiators are involved. According to the negotiation dilemma, the better the agreements get, the harder it is to achieve an agreement, leading to a decrease in the agreement rate.

Table 5   Comparison of Medians Across Matching Combinations for Dyadic Variables
          (*Agreements Only)

	H2	H3a	H3b	H4
Matching/Dependent Variables	Agreement Rate	Joint Utility*	Distance to Pareto-frontier*	Contract Imbalance*
None (N=11)	84.6%	108.0%	3.0pp	8.0pp
One (N=22)	81.5%	110.0%	3.0pp	5.5pp
Both (N=12)	80.0%	111.0%	3.0pp	5.0pp

Matching trainings and learning styles have no effect on the agreement rate ($\chi^2(2)$=0.104, p=0.949). Also, the underlying variables learning style and training method show no effect if evaluated separately. Thus, hypothesis 2 is not supported.

Detailed data analysis of negotiation efficiency is performed using a Kruskal-Wallis test. Regarding joint utility (H(2)=2.393, p=0.303) and the distance of an agreement to the Pareto-frontier (H(2)=0.937, p=0.626), no significant effects of personalised trainings can be found. Thus, hypotheses 3a and 3b are not supported. However, median values (cf. Table 5) and means (cf. Figure 9) confirm the matching assumption showing increasing joint utility the more matches are involved and decreasing distance to the Pareto-optimal agreement.

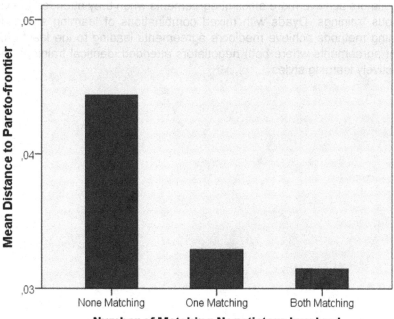

Figure 9   Average Distance to Pareto-Frontier on Number of Matching Negotiators per Negotiation

Again, combinations of training methods, learning styles and interaction effects are analysed in negotiation dyads using a two-way independent

ANOVA. To keep group sizes large, only equal versus unequal combinations of training methods and practical versus mixed versus theoretical combinations of learning styles are analysed. Because group sizes are unequal η^2 is calculated to report effect sizes (Levine and Hullett 2002). However, the data reveals no effect of learning styles or interaction effect, but a significant effect of the combination of training methods on joint utility $(F(1,39)=5.633, p=0.023, \eta^2_{training\ method}=0.00014^*)$ and distance to the Pareto-frontier $(F(1,39)=6.846, p=0.013, \eta^2_{training\ method}=0.055^*)$.

Regarding joint utility and the distance to the Pareto-frontier, the data confirms the matching assumption (cf. Figure 10). Negotiation dyads containing practical negotiators achieve more efficient agreements when they attended the enactive trainings. Negotiation dyads containing theoretical negotiators achieve more efficient agreements when they attended the vicarious trainings. Dyads with mixed combinations of learning styles or training methods achieve mediocre agreements leading to the least efficient agreements where both negotiators attended identical trainings respectively learning styles.

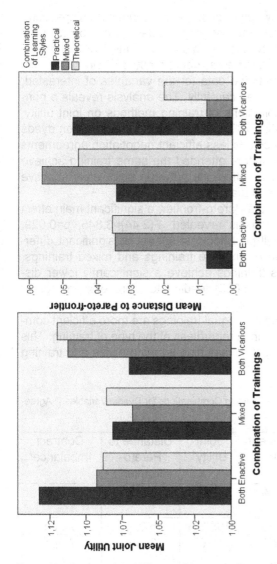

Figure 10   Average Joint Utility and Distance to Pareto-Frontier on Combinations of Training Methods

Analysing the differences between enactive and vicarious trainings alone a one-way ANOVA is conducted to assess the effect of combinations of training methods on joint utility and the distance to the Pareto-frontier. However, ANOVA, often described as a robust method (Field 2013), disregards the not normally distributed data for the variables of interested, thus results have to be interpreted carefully. The analysis reveals a non-significant effect of the combinations of training methods on joint utility, $F(2,44)=3.054$, $p=0.058$, $\eta^2=0.127$. Table 6 shows that negotiation dyads attending different trainings achieve less efficient negotiation agreements while dyads where both negotiators attended the same training achieve more efficient agreements. The difference between completely enactive and vicarious dyads, however, is marginal.

Analysing the distance to the Pareto-frontier, a significant main effect of the combinations of trainings is revealed, $F(2,44)=3.845$, $p=0.029$, $\eta^2=0.155^*$. The Games-Howell post-hoc test shows no significant difference between a combination of enactive trainings and mixed trainings. However, dyads of vicarious trainings achieve a significantly lower distance to the Pareto-frontier ($p=0.039$) leading to more efficient agreements.

Overall, negotiation dyads with equal trainings are more efficient compared to dyads with mixed trainings regardless of the type of training. This effect is stronger than the effect of matching learning styles and training methods regarding its size.

Table 6   Medians across End-User Training Combinations for Dyadic Variables (* Agreements Only)

EUT/Dependent Variables	Agreement Rate	Joint Utility*	Distance to Pareto-frontier*	Contract Imbalance*
Both enactive (N=13)	86.7%	111.0%	3.0pp	7.0pp
Mixed (N=23)	85.2%	108.0%	5.8pp	7.0pp
Both vicarious (N=9)	69.2%	111.0%	3.0pp	7.0pp

In accordance with the ANOVA, comparing the effects of learning style, training method, and relevant interaction effects, the analysis of learning styles reveals no further effects on joint utility or the distance to the Pareto-frontier.

   Regarding the hypothesised positive effect of matching learning style and training method on the fairness of the agreements measured by contract imbalance the data reveals no significant effect (H(2)=4.355, p=0.113) which leads us to reject hypothesis 4. Follow-up analyses (Bonferroni correction is marked by plus-sign [+]) showed a slight increase in fairness of the negotiated agreements from non-matching dyads to dyads with one matching negotiator (Mdn_{none}= 0.080, Mdn_{mixed}= 0.055, U=75.00, p=0.246[+], r=0.308) as well as from dyads with one matching negotiator to all-matching dyads (Mdn_{mixed}= 0.055, Mdn_{both}= 0.050, U=128.50, p=0.899[+], r=0.022) leading to a medium improvement of negotiation fairness comparing non-matching with all-matching negotiation dyads (Mdn_{none}= 0.080, Mdn_{both}= 0.050, U=34.00, p=0.153[+], r=0.414). A two-way-independent ANOVA did not reveal further main or interaction effects of contract imbalance on learning styles or training methods.

2.6   Discussion

Although most effects are statistically insignificant, the assumed tendencies for all hypotheses exist, mostly supporting our theoretical argumentation integrating learning styles, negotiation styles, and behaviour. The data shows that negotiators preferring theoretical learning styles on average follow an avoiding negotiation style with some competitive behaviour leading to fewer but more efficient and fairer agreements exchanging few messages. Negotiators with practical learning styles behaved more cooperative or accommodating leading to a high amount of less efficient and unfair agreements exchanging numerous messages. In such dyads especially, practical negotiators were exploited by their counterparts leading to lower individual utilities. In contrast to our argumentation based on Ma et al. (2012), practical negotiators achieve lower individual outcomes being less assertive than expected compared to theoretical negotiators.

   Regarding hypotheses 1a and 1b, there is a strong tendency that personalised trainings enable negotiators to acquire e-negotiation skills more easily (cf. Table 7). This effect is stronger for e-negotiation skill acquisition than for face-to-face negotiation skill acquisition, which might be due to the focus of the EUT on e-negotiations. Matching training methods and learning styles neither affect negotiation effectiveness, efficiency nor fairness leading us to reject hypotheses 2 – 4. Nevertheless, the data confirms our description of strengths and weaknesses of the different learning styles showing tendencies that negotiators with a matching training by tendency achieved fairer negotiation agreements. In contrast to our argumentation in section 2.3.2, the increased number of messages in practical dyads did not hinder but improve efficiency. The data shows an even stronger effect of equal trainings or equal learning styles leading to more efficient outcomes. Using the SVO to explain our results means that practical negotiators use more relationship-focused tactics aiming for cooperation, whilst theoretical negotiators use a mix of relation and task-oriented tactics (Olekalns and Smith 1999). Combining two negotiators of the same style produces an equally efficient dyad, while mixing both approaches leads to a strong focus on task-orientation, which is less efficient regarding negotiation outcomes.

Table 7   Summary of Hypotheses

	Evaluation	Significance level	Effect size	Follow-up
H1a	Not supported	p=0.185	r=0.127	-
H1b	Supported	p=0.023	r=0.216*	-
H2	Not supported	ns	V=0.043	-
H3a	Not supported	ns	$r_{none/both}$=0.318	Equal trainings better (η^2=0.127)
H3b	Not supported	ns	$r_{none/both}$=0.191	Equal trainings better (η^2=0.155*)
H4	Not supported	p=0.113	$r_{none/both}$=0.414	Comparing none/both matching (r=0.414)

Firstly, this study confirms the assumption that a matching between learning style and training method improves acquisition and application of skills. Secondly, it shows a strong impact of the coordination of such styles and training methods in negotiations as collaborative work processes making negotiation dyads with equal trainings or learning styles more efficient.

In line with previous research (Gupta and Anson 2014; Ben-Yoav and Banai 1992; Robey and Taggart 1983), the effects of individual differences or learning styles as a measure of individual differences are very small and often superposed by other influences, e.g. culture. Besides their volatile effects, learning styles (especially the LSQ) are also intertwined with theories on culture sharing similar constructs e.g. the dimension of assertiveness closely-related to uncertainty tolerance in culture studies (Hofstede 1984).

There is also an effect of habituation to prevalent training methods. Since theoretical teaching is the standard at both participating universities the vicarious training leads to higher skill acquisition, although, according to the literature, there is no superior training method in general (Gupta et al. 2010). The superiority of equal training methods or learning styles over mixed ones confirms the findings of other studies that learning styles often influence learning outcomes rather by interaction effects with the training method than directly (Gupta and Anson 2014). In negotiations such effects can be explained focusing on the contents of the trainings, or simply the familiarity:

1) Training method and learning style could influence the negotiation behaviour facilitating either a relationship-oriented or task-oriented negotiation strategy making equal dyads more efficient (Olekalns and Smith 1999).

2) Simply the familiarity with the partners' behaviour could lead to a mutual understanding when negotiating with a counterpart that attended an identical training or prefers the same learning style reducing the cognitive load required to encode such behaviour (Sweller 1994).

The present study is limited by the small sample size (i.e. 110 negotiators in 55 negotiation dyads) especially if splitting the sample into groups according to their training method or learning style becomes necessary, restricting the statistical methods that can be used. Another limitation is the specific distribution of learning styles in the dataset as the sample is not distributed equally among all four learning styles (Allinson and Hayes 1988). Furthermore, we only used the most preferred learning style of each participant disregarding the interval-scaled preference values produced by the LSQ (Duff and Duffy 2002). Although previous studies on training methods found effects performing similarly short 2-hour trainings (Thompson 1990), the analysis of learning styles obviously requires a large amount of dedicated training to induce effects compared to predominant conceptions of learning acquired over a semester or even several years of studies. The time-period of about one week between the trainings and the subsequent negotiation as well as the group work performed in the enactive training bringing together learners with different styles, might have blurred the findings making it hard to bridge the distance between personalised learning and the application of this knowledge, consequently diminishing effect sizes.

2.7 Conclusion

The current paper provides an application of theories of personalised EUTs to the domain of NSSs. Following its research aim, two personalised EUTs have been developed and evaluated addressing individual learning styles by providing matching training methods. The approach can be generalised to NSSs per se and even to ISs. The personalised trainings have been evaluated performing a negotiation experiment. However, similar to existing research on individual differences in various domains, the effects of such differences are often small. Effects of personalised EUTs on acquisition of electronic negotiation skills, negotiation efficiency, and fairness of the agreements could be measured. Training methods have stronger effects on the outcome variables measured than learning styles. Also, negotiations with partners who received an identical training or prefer the identical learning style have been found to be more efficient.

This implies for practitioners that knowing your own style as well as your negotiation partner(s)' style(s) affects negotiation outcomes. The effects of learners being informed of their individual learning style need to be analysed following management education, where personal styles are deliberately used to induce processes of self-reflection (Shell 2001).

Implications for researchers include the improvement of the experimental procedure, and a greater focus on SCT facilitating social and/or cognitive aspects. Firstly, researchers carefully need to adapt and improve the experimental procedure to be able to identify moderating variables for explaining the connection between learning styles and negotiation styles taking into account their common ancestors. One possibility to strengthen the connection between learning styles and negotiation styles is to adapt the LSQ instrument to the domain of negotiations. As individual differences are dynamic constructs being hard to measure, a more domain specific questionnaire can be promising. Secondly, a greater focus on social aspects needs to switch the object of analysis from negotiation dyads to group decision-making or computer-supported collaborative work processes including more than two participants. However, this poses several challenges regarding sample size, moderating variables and matchings of learning styles and training methods. Finally, a greater focus on the cognitive aspects can also mean a change of the object of analysis investigating personalised learning from a task perspective. Cognitive theories, such as cognitive load (Sweller 1988) or cognitive fit (Vessey 1991) usually investigate the mental representation of problem solving tasks similar to learning processes. Thus, analysing learning or negotiation tasks on a more granular level could be a promising avenue being able to observe actual task-related behaviour of participants instead of measuring their potentially biased perceptions. However, such analyses require an extension of cognitive theories from the individual level to at least bilateral processes. First steps into this direction have been reported extending cognitive fit to interdependent tasks (Shaft and Vessey 2006).

3 A Conceptual Framework for Task and Tool Personalisation in IS Education

Abstract
Learner-centred, self-regulated learning approaches such as flipped class-rooms or personalised learning environments (PLEs) are popular. This paper analyses personalised learning in collaborative, self-regulated e-learning approaches applying the theory of cognitive fit to explain the personalisation of learning tasks and learning tools. The PLF is presented defining the core constructs of such learning processes as well as a method of personalisation. The feasibility of the framework is demonstrated using a thought experiment describing its possible application to a university course on electronic negotiations as part of an IS curriculum. Current learning methods used in the course and new learning methods matching the PLF are compared and discussed critically, identifying potentials to improve personalised learning as well as avenues for personalised learning research.

Co-Author
Prof. Mareike Schoop, PhD

Re-publication of this article is performed with permission of the Association of Information Systems. The original article has been published in: Proceedings of the International Conference on Information Systems (ICIS) 2015, A Conceptual Framework for Task and Tool Personalisation in IS Education, 2015, IS Curriculum and Education, paper 6, Philipp Melzer, Mareike Schoop, available at http://aisel.aisnet.org/icis2015/proceedings/ISedu/6/

© Springer Fachmedien Wiesbaden GmbH, part of Springer Nature 2019
P. Melzer, *A Conceptual Framework for Personalised Learning*,
https://doi.org/10.1007/978-3-658-23095-1_3

3.1   Introduction

In recent years, the importance of e-learning has increased leading to a convergence of technological and pedagogical innovation aiming for educational goals supported by technology (Garrison 2011). Conforming to Dewey (1997, p.46) who noted that teachers are

> "concerned with providing conditions so adapted to individual needs and powers as to make for the permanent improvement of observation, suggestion, and investigation",

the importance of personalised learning has been recognised in research and practice. Personalisation by a teacher, however, is only possible in small classes mostly relying on face-to-face learning. To enable automatic personalisation, new methods using expert systems or data mining approaches are employed leading to high investments in start-ups developing and applying such technologies (Emerson 2013). According to the learning paradigm of constructivism (Kafai 2006), only learners themselves are truly able to regulate their learning processes. Such learner-centred, self-regulated approaches (such as learning in informal settings directly at the workplace or flipped classrooms) are getting more and more popular shifting responsibilities for organising the learning process from teachers to learners (Tsai et al. 2013). Self-regulated personalisation not only includes time and pace but the definition of learning objectives and even learning tasks to achieve these objectives. Such personalisation, however, requires a certain awareness based on a profound evaluation of one's own skills and learning preferences (Zimmerman 1989).

PLEs strive to support personalisation in self-regulated learning. In contrast to VLEs, PLEs are not single systems but user-configured sets of interchangeable social media (formerly Web 2.0) tools such as blogs, wikis, media sharing services, podcasts, social networks, or social bookmarking services (Attwell 2007). Due to their ubiquitous availability, conjunction to private use, and independence of learning institutions, PLEs are easy to set up and to use for individuals as well as for groups of learners. However, configuration, usage, and evaluation of social media tools in the context of PLEs requires digital literacy and awareness (McLoughlin and Lee 2010):

1) Although there is an increasing expectation that learners as digital natives already possess digital literacy through the permanent engagement with social media, there is also a strong need for explicit scaffolding as learners might not know how to use such technologies for learning or see their relevance for learning (Katz and Macklin 2007);

2) Constant private use of social media might also affect their behaviour adversely leading to impatience or an overly casual approach to learning (CLEX 2009).

Both problems, i.e. the matching of learning preferences to learning tasks as well as to learning tools, can be generalised to the class of matching problems which has been the topic of numerous studies in the IS domain (e.g. Gupta and Anson 2014; Robey and Taggart 1981) and the learning sciences (e.g. Kolb and Kolb 2005; Vermunt 1996). Although different kinds of cognitive styles or learning styles have been analysed with different kinds of learning methods or IS designs, matches have rarely been found. Until today, there is no consistent theory that is able to explain such matching processes (Coffield et al. 2004; Pashler et al. 2009).

The research goal of this work is thus to explain and support self-regulated personalisation, matching learning preferences to learning tasks and PLE tools. In contrast to previous attempts to demonstrate specific matches between learning styles and learning methods or contents, this paper focuses on learning tasks as the construct of personalisation which is defined by the learners themselves providing an alternative method to define such matches. Therefore, this paper aims to provide an overview of the heterogeneous theories of learning and cognitive fit (Vessey 1991) in section 3.2 and integrate them into the PLF showing the main influence factors for collaborative, self-regulated personalised learning in section 3.3. In section 3.4, the feasibility of the PLF will be demonstrated by a thought experiment, applying it to an example university course which is part of an IS curriculum. The paper concludes with a discussion and an outlook to future work.

3.2 Theoretical Foundations

The following section presents a literature review of the theories shaping the PLF, integrating collaborative e-learning, personalised learning and cognitive fit.

3.2.1   Collaborative Electronic Learning

Several learning paradigms existing in the learning sciences are applied to e-learning, defining how learners acquire knowledge (cf. Figure 11). Instructivism focuses on a teacher standing in front of the class transmitting knowledge to the learners. Whilst behaviourism (Skinner 1958) follows a stimuli-response model where the human mind is modelled as a black box, cognitivism (Tennyson 1992) particularly investigates this black box modelling human memory. Cognitivism thereby focuses on the information processing taking place along the transmission of knowledge. In contrast to instructivism, constructivism (Jonassen 1990) defines learning as the construction of knowledge by the learners using observation and reflective thinking. There are two major streams within constructivism, namely situated learning in communities of practice (Lave and Wenger 1991), (aiming to explore authentic problems) and constructionism (Kafai 2006) (which explicitly emphasises social aspects such as learning in groups describing learning as an inseparable relationship between personal meaning making and social influences) (Garrison 2011). Through social interaction between teachers and learners as well as among learners, ideas are communicated, and knowledge is constructed and confirmed. Learners, therefore, have an important responsibility to manage the learning process and achieve their learning goals while teachers merely assist this process.

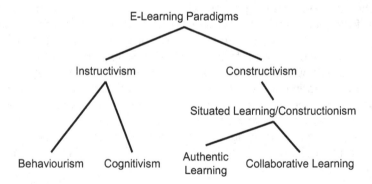

Figure 11   Taxonomy of E-Learning Paradigms (adapted from Melzer and Schoop 2014c, p.780)

To reflect the inherent connection of e-learning and constructionism, this paper follows the definition of Garrison describing e-learning as "electronically mediated asynchronous and synchronous communication for the purpose of constructing and confirming knowledge" (Garrison 2011, p.2).

This is performed in Communities of Inquiry (COIs). The COI framework (cf. Figure 12) defines cognitive presence, social presence, and teaching presence as key dimensions providing guidelines for implementing and evaluating constructionist e-learning courses. *Cognitive presence* describes the individual perception and acquisition of new knowledge, skills and abilities through critical discourse and application to a problem domain. *Social presence* represents the transfer of these individual efforts to a group of learners. COIs focus on asynchronous exchange of text messages to enable collaboration. This type of electronically mediated communication is described to be particularly effective in facilitating critical discourse providing users with more time to think through their utterances systematically and to document all statements making them public to the COI. Sustainable and cohesive groups of learners are particularly important to facilitate discourse providing each individual with the opportunity to discuss and confirm individual knowledge as well as to help other learners. *Teaching presence* represents the influence of the teacher moderating discourse ensuring an open climate assisting the learning process. At the same time, the teacher is responsible for selecting and preparing the learning contents according to the course goals to facilitate information processing adhering to the learners' preferences. Thereby learners need to be enabled to regulate and personalise their learning experience themselves. Overall, these three heavily intertwined dimensions represent the core of constructionist e-learning.

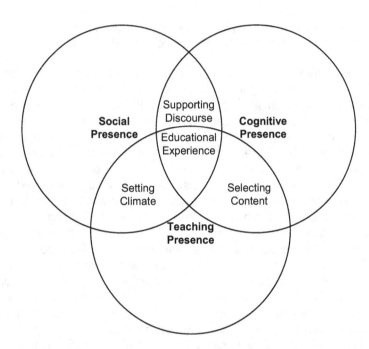

Figure 12   Community of inquiry Theoretical Research Framework (Garrison 2011, p.23)

3.2.2   Personalised Learning

Personalised learning can be structured into two dimensions:

1) Who is responsible for the personalisation – a teacher or learning system on the one hand or the learners themselves on the other hand;
2) What is going to be personalised – learning methods or learning content.

Following constructionism, a learner-centred approach to personalisation is pursued. Thereby, the paper focuses on personalisation of the learning method in a self-regulated fashion, keeping the learning contents constant.

Personalised learning is usually related to individual characteristics and abilities of the learners. The work of Jung on personality types (Jung 1923) has led to numerous theories and instruments on learning styles

(Coffield et al. 2004). They can be structured from largely constitutionally-based factors to concrete learning approaches, strategies, orientations, and conceptions. Each learning style is supposed to fit certain learning environments, methods, or scenarios. Personality-based factors have been a topic in IS research, analysing cognitive styles in IS usage patterns (e.g. Robey and Taggart 1981; Taggart et al. 1982) or learning styles in EUTs (e.g. Davis and Bostrom 199; Melzer and Schoop 2014b). Several matches between learning styles and learning methods have been proposed. However, many learning style instruments lack validation and findings are seldom reproduced due to small effect sizes and numerous confounding variables. Thus, the value of using personality traits in the design and usage of IS has been questioned (e.g. Gupta and Anson 2014; Huber 1983).

3.2.3 Cognitive Fit

The theory of cognitive fit (Vessey 1991) emerged from the debate whether graphical or tabular problem-solving tasks fit specific mental representations of how to solve these tasks. Emphasising information processing theory, it created the theoretical foundations to match *mental representations for a task-solution* to *problem-solving tasks,* proposing a consistent mental representation in human memory to decrease complexity leading to a better *problem-solving performance.* Over the years, the model of cognitive fit has been extended (cf. Figure 13) to grasp more detail including an *internal representation of the problem domain* as well as an *external problem representation* (Shaft and Vessey 2006). While the internal representation refers to knowledge about the meaning of symbols or mathematical procedures which has to be retrieved from memory, the external representation refers to shapes and positions of symbols on paper or other media which can be retrieved from the environment. Both the internal and external representation influence each other leading to a mental representation for task-solution. Cognitive fit has already been applied to interdependent tasks in the domain of software engineering (Shaft and Vessey 2006). An analysis of the interwoven software maintenance tasks of code comprehension and code modification showed how cognitive fit can be used to explain and integrate effects on the overall problem.

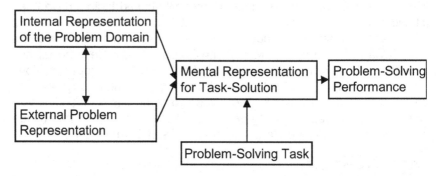

Figure 13   Extended Cognitive Fit Model (Shaft and Vessey 2006, p.32)

Vessey and Galletta emphasise the importance of tasks as the unit of analysis referring to the debate on cognitive styles:

> "Rather than seeking measures of cognitive style in an attempt to explain the incremental effects of individual differences on performance, we suggest seeking *information processing skills that support a particular task* [...]" (Vessey and Galletta 1991, p.69)

We, therefore, use cognitive fit as a new approach to personalised learning arguing that the self-regulated personalisation of learning tasks and PLE tools are two parallel but interdependent processes of cognitive fit, where the learners have to match their representations of the respective learning problem to specific learning tasks and learning tools. Achieving such a fit in one or both matching processes should increase learning performance. Following the idea of cognitive fit, personalised learning can be analysed focusing on the configuration, management, and evaluation of learning tasks as well as learning tools to infer preferences and predict learning performance. However, a clear-cut taxonomy of learning tasks and learning tools is necessary to define possible matches.

3.2.4   Taxonomy of Learning Tasks

Bloom's taxonomy of learning objectives (Bloom et al. 1984), one of the most prominent taxonomies in the learning sciences, defines learning tasks together with specific levels of knowledge as a two-dimensional allocation of learning objectives in its revised version (Anderson and Krathwohl 2001). The knowledge dimension differentiates knowledge on facts, concepts, or procedures from metacognitive knowledge (i.e. knowing about one's own knowledge). In self-regulated learning through web-based systems, such metacognitive knowledge is particularly important because it is used to organise and personalise the learning experience (Narciss et al. 2007). Knowledge can be acquired performing different cognitive processes grouped in ascending order of complexity from lower order thinking skills (i.e. remembering, understanding, and applying) to higher order thinking skills (i.e. analysing, evaluating, and creating). Courses typically encompass several learning objectives combining cognitive processes and knowledge levels. The taxonomy, furthermore, defines specific learning tasks, which can be used to achieve these learning objectives for every cognitive process (cf. Table 8). Bloom's taxonomy shows its cognitivist roots as a tool for teachers to structure their classes only describing knowledge acquisition omitting constructionist learning tasks focusing on situated learning or collaboration.

Table 8   Cognitive Process and Learning Tasks (based on Krathwohl 2002, pp.214-215; Churches 2009)

Cognitive Processes	Complexity	Learning Tasks	Digital Learning Tasks
Remember		Recognising, Recalling	Bullet pointing, Highlighting, Bookmarking, Social networking, Social bookmarking, Favouriting/Local bookmarking, Searching,
Understand	Lower Order Thinking Skills	Interpreting, Exemplifying, Classifying, Summarising, Inferring, Comparing, Explaining,	Advanced Searches, Boolean searches, Blog journaling, Twittering, Categorising, Tagging, Commenting, Annotating, Subscribing
Apply		Executing, Implementing	Running, Loading, Playing, Operating, Hacking, Uploading, Sharing, Editing
Analyse		Differentiating, Organising, Attributing	Mashing, Linking, Validating, Reverse engineering, Cracking, Media Clipping
Evaluate	Higher Order Thinking Skills	Checking, Critiquing	Blog commenting, Reviewing, Posting, Moderating, Collaborating, Networking, Refactoring, Testing
Create		Generating, Planning, Producing	Programming, Filming, Animating, Blogging, Video blogging, Mixing, Wikiing, Publishing, Videocasting, Podcasting, Directing

Churches (2009) applies Bloom's taxonomy to digital learning extending it by learning tasks performed in digital environments using social media tools as well as including the notion of collaboration inherent to social media. Remembering can, therefore, be supported digitally by highlighting words in a text, building a social network to ask experts, or searching and bookmarking resources on the web, while understanding is facilitated by advanced searches using complex expressions, journaling contents in (micro)-blogs, categorising or tagging it. Application tasks represent lower as well as higher order thinking skills including running a software and especially sharing content over media sharing services. Higher order thinking skills such as analysis and evaluation include the mashing up, reverse engineering, commenting, or refactoring of content in blogs focusing, for example, on reports and their assessment. Finally, the creation of content, as a main goal of social media, includes the complete generation and publishing of programs, videos, wikis, podcasts etc. on the web (cf. Table 8).

3.2.5 Taxonomy of Learning Tools

Promoting openness, interoperability, and user control (Siemens 2007), PLEs reflect the idea of social media. In contrast to VLEs, they represent an approach rather than a specific application where learners can create, share, mash-up, and discuss content using the tools they prefer (Downes 2005). Since PLEs by no means restrict the social media tools which can be used, and technological evolution still produces numerous new kinds of tools, the definition of an exhaustive taxonomy of tools is impossible. Thus, we focus on the most prominent types of tools which are used within PLEs, namely microblogging services, social bookmarking services, podcasts, blogs, wikis, mind maps, video sharing platforms, and image creation services (Attwell 2007; Siemens 2007).

Such tools are configured and used within PLEs for two reasons:

1) customisation of the learning environment providing ownership, control, and literacy and
2) social support through collaboration with a learning group or across boundaries with practitioners facilitating the learning process (Buchem et al. 2011).

Supporting the individual dimensions ownership and control, learners will be enabled to design and manage their learning processes breaking down learning objectives into learning tasks based on individual learning preferences. Personalisation of tools thus is guided by the learning tasks required to achieve the learning objectives (Bower et al. 2010; Churches 2009). Bower et al. (2010), consequently, propose a framework of social media learning designs assigning social media learning tasks to Bloom's taxonomy of learning objectives defining how specific social media tools can be used to achieve certain learning objectives following a construc-tionist perspective (cf. Table 9). It must be noted that Table 9 only shows a reduced version of social media tools for the sake of clarity, omitting the concrete learning tasks that have to be defined w.r.t. a specific learning content. The allocation of tools shows that social media facilitates the idea of constructionism by numerous possibilities to create contents collabora-tively. Regarding the knowledge dimension, microblogging and social bookmarking services match the acquisition of factual knowledge while wikis provide conceptual knowledge. Video-related tools such as recording software, podcasts, and media sharing are especially suitable to acquire procedural knowledge. Finally, mind maps and blogs focus on metacogni-tive knowledge. The more constructive a tool is, the better it facilitates higher order thinking skills (Bower et al. 2010).

Table 9　Framework of Social Media Learning Designs (adapted from Bower et al. 2010, pp. 190-191)

The Knowledge Dimension	The Cognitive Process					
	Remember	Understand	Apply	Analyse	Evaluate	Create
Factual Knowledge	Microblog	Social Bookmarking, Podcast	Image Creation	Wiki	Social Bookmarking, Blog	Image Creation
Conceptual Knowledge	Wiki, Podcast	Blog, Wiki, Mind map	Video	Wiki, Podcast	Wiki, Blog	Mind map
Procedural Knowledge	Video, Podcast	Podcast	Blog, Video	Video	Blog, Video	Image Creation
Metacognitive Knowledge	Mind map	Mind map	Blog	Blog	Blog	Mind map

3.3   The Personalised Learning Framework

This section aims to integrate the heterogeneous theories described in the previous sections into the PLF to explain the process of personalised learning. Reflecting constructionism inherently involving collaborative learning, the source of the PLF is not an individual learner, but a community of inquiry (COI). Although an inherent property of personalisation is its focus on individuality, personalisation of tasks and tools in constructionist learning occurs in groups considering the process of learning equally important than the learning outcomes. Therefore, individuals have to negotiate their preferred tasks and tools with their peers and teachers to find a consensus. The core framework (cf. Figure 14) thus contains the COI personalising learning tasks and learning tools. Matching learning preferences of the learners to respective tasks and tools are modelled as cognitive fit processes.

The analysis of personality traits as learning styles typically treats such styles as fairly stable. Literature on personality-based learning styles, however, shows that there are numerous contextual variables that often outshine personality traits and thus have to be considered in the framework (Pashler et al. 2009). Classroom contextual factors such as learning styles, for example, are criticised for their often normative nature. Defined and assessed by a teacher, a non-preferred style might lead to disadvantages for the learner (Pintrich et al. 1993). Looking at informal learning scenarios, learning motivation differs greatly. Learning goals need to be balanced between personal life, work life, and other interests. A part-time learner's motivation is often non-comparable to that of a full-time learner (Haggis 2003).

Most of the time, PLEs are taken to be completely learner-driven environments, exceeding the learning goals of a single course being available for further learning. However, the PLF adheres to the narrow definition of PLEs adhering to a learning institution to

"enable self-direction, knowledge building, and autonomy by providing options and choice while still supplying the necessary structure and scaffolding." (McLoughlin and Lee 2010, p.33).

If applied to a real university course, the learning institution's strategy and culture as well as its infrastructure will affect learning. A university's strategy is transferred to the staff and eventually to the students reflecting the country's culture as well as a learning culture.

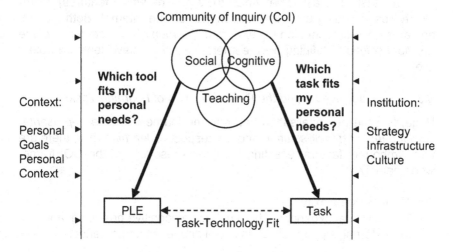

Figure 14   Conceptual Framework of Requirements for Personalised Learning

3.3.1   Cognitive Fit and Personalised Learning

The PLF shows that the personalisation of learning tasks and learning tools are two interdependent processes of cognitive fit. Learners personalise their learning experience throughout the learning process configuring, managing, and evaluating tasks and tools to achieve their desired learning objectives, at the same time acquiring awareness and digital literacy for further learning processes (Narciss et al. 2007).

Learning awareness is an important prerequisite to personalisation in self-regulated learning. In the model of cognitive fit, learning awareness is represented as *internal representation of the learning domain* as well as *external representation of the learning domain*. The internal representation contains experiences, feelings, and thoughts (i.e. which tools do I like to use; how do I want to break down a learning objective into learning tasks?). The internal representation can be guided by personality traits or learning preferences. The problem here is to retrieve and explicate such information to make it accessible and understandable, which requires experience. The external representation encompasses material such as written text or guidance by peers that present information increasing the learning awareness (i.e. what tasks are available; which tools provide which features). Complexity lies in finding such information e.g. on the Internet. Both internal and external representation together form the *mental representation of the task/tool-solution*, defining how learners want to achieve learning objectives.

3.3.2   Cognitive Fit and the Personalisation of Learning Tasks

Regarding the personalisation between the learners' *mental representation of a learning task-solution* and the respective *learning task*, there are three important factors reflecting the three presences of the COI framework, namely

1)   task complexity,
2)   individual experience, both reflecting cognitive presence, and
3)   external support reflecting social and teaching presence.

The concrete learning tasks complexity must match the complexity of the learner's problem representation (i.e. the *mental representation of a learning task-solution*). Cognitive fit demonstrated that achieving a fit between a task and a mental representation of a problem reduces mental complexity and thus increases problem-solving performance. The presented taxonomy of learning tasks distinguishes learning task complexity into lower order and higher order thinking skills. Performing overly complex tasks leads to overburdened learners who are unable to execute the learning task, while performing overly easy tasks leads to ineffective learning. To break down learning objectives into matching learning tasks regarding their complexity, individual experience is an important factor. In the domain of cognitive fit, higher information processing skills (e.g. through experience) for a specific decision-making task as well as task and problem combination have been demonstrated to increase decision-making performance (Vessey and Galletta 1991). Such metacognitive knowledge about previously performed learning tasks, contents, or individual preferences demonstrates the internal representation. The social constructionist notion of PLEs can also help to create such knowledge by engaging in discussions with peers or teachers to confirm or dismiss knowledge collaboratively fostering the exchange between internal and external knowledge of the learning domain. Achieving a cognitive fit between this *mental representation of the task-solution* and the *learning task* represents an optimally personalised learning task.

3.3.3 Cognitive Fit and the Personalisation of Learning Tools

A similar process takes place regarding the PLE tools used to achieve learning objectives. However, these tools cannot achieve learning objectives alone, but support specific learning tasks. Therefore, the learners have to match their *mental representation of learning tool-solution* to a specific *learning task supported by a learning tool*. There are several matches of tasks (e.g. discussion) to tools (e.g. social networks) leading to a task-technology fit while other combinations do not match. Predictors of task-technology either reside within the tasks' or technologies' characteristics (Goodhue and Thompson 1995). Task-related predictors facilitating fit are performing routine tasks, few task interdependences, and power to define and orchestrate the tasks themselves. While the PLF fosters the hand-over of responsibilities to the learners to create such openness, learning is seldom focusing on easy routine tasks. Technology-related predictors are the experience of the user with a specific software and the departmental background, both pointing out the necessity of digital literacy. However, it is assumed that achieving a cognitive fit in the personalisation of learning tools implicitly leads to a task-technology fit, since the learning tasks influence both processes. Investigating cognitive fit, analyses have been conducted w.r.t. tools supporting the decision process (e.g. structured English, decision tables or decision trees) in programming tasks. Cognitive fit could show specific matching conditions that increased performance (Vessey and Weber 1986).

We will complement these findings from a learning perspective, analysing the PLE-tool-selection-process, which depends on the

1) overarching learning objectives and outcomes,
2) respective dimensions of knowledge and cognitive processes expected,
3) type of pedagogy applied, and
4) preferred modalities of representation (Bower et al. 2010).

This confirms the importance of a clear communication of learning objectives and the freedom and awareness to deconstruct them to concrete learning tasks to achieve learning outcomes. Digital literacy is also important, referring to the internal representation, to know which PLE tools enable which learning outcomes. Regarding the type of pedagogy, however, social media tools particularly support higher order thinking skills such as the creation of contents in blogs or wikis. Finally, learners can influence the preferred mode of presentation choosing for example blogs over image creation. Achieving a cognitive fit between this *mental representation of the learning tool-solution* and the *learning task supported by a learning tool* represents an optimally personalised learning tool.

3.3.4   Synthesis of the Personalisation of Tasks and Tools

The analysis of cognitive fit in interdependent processes proposes that both personalisation of learning tasks and personalisation of learning tools run in parallel for each sub-task (Shaft and Vessey 2006). The resulting *mental representations of the learning task-solution* and *mental representation of the learning tool-solution* are then integrated into one *mental representation for personalised learning* again requiring a fit, consequently leading to improved *learning performance*. Increasing learning awareness via the facilitation of constant (re-)evaluation of the *internal representation* as well as *external representation* enables the learners to achieve cognitive fit regarding their *mental representation of the learning task-solution*, *mental representation of the learning tool-solution*, and, consequently, the *mental representation of personalised learning* increasing *learning performance* (cf. Figure 15). Learning performance is thus defined as the degree to which the learning outcomes fulfil the learning objectives. In a constructionist learning experience, learning outcomes can be divided into cognitive, affective, and psychomotor outcomes (Bloom et al. 1984). However, this paper focuses primarily on the cognitive outcomes.

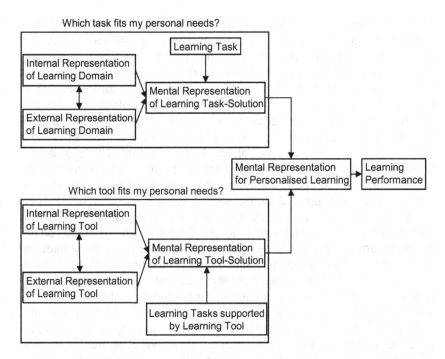

Figure 15   Cognitive Fit in Personalised Learning (adapted from Shaft and Vessey 2006, p.33)

3.4   An Example Application of the Personalised Learning Framework

The feasibility of the PLF is demonstrated by applying it to an actual university course ANM in a thought experiment. First, the status quo of teaching in ANM is described leading to a detailed description of learning methods used and contents taught. We will then present the application of the PLF to ANM, resulting in a new course with the identical content and learning objectives but with different learning methods facilitating collaborative learning and self-regulated personalisation.

3.4.1   Teaching Electronic Negotiations in Information Systems

Negotiations represent complex management tasks comprising of interdependent communication and decision-making processes (Bichler et al.

2003). As such, they are often included in IS or business administration curricula in higher education preparing students for their jobs. Electronic communication media such as e-mail are increasingly used for negotiations, although they possess certain obstacles which inhibit optimal negotiation performance (Schoop et al. 2008). For example, communication is unstructured; archiving of messages is left to the negotiators; and decision-making in multi-attributive negotiations is challenging. Electronic negotiations are defined as negotiations supported by electronic means providing additional support features (Ströbel and Weinhardt 2003). NSSs, as archetypes of ISs, aim to support human negotiators providing communication support, decision support, document management, and further support functionalities (Schoop et al. 2003; Schoop 2010).

Negotiation pedagogy in management education largely focuses on instructivist face-to-face courses (Lewicki 1997). E-learning courses on negotiations are scarce, providing web-based trainings that mainly follow instructivism sometimes including simulations (Eliashberg et al. 1992; Kaufman 1998). Nevertheless, the necessity of combining conceptual and procedural knowledge is acknowledged by employing explicit examples, case studies, negotiation experts, or negotiation simulations (Loewenstein and Thompson 2006). Practicing the use of NSSs additionally requires e-negotiation-related content such as electronic communication media, specific support features, and experience in using NSSs. In electronic negotiation courses, learner motivation is usually very high facilitating self-regulated learning approaches (Köszegi and Kersten 2003). Because of the collaborative nature of negotiations, the process of negotiation itself is often seen as a collaborative learning task (Andriessen 2006).

3.4.2   Advanced Negotiation Management: Status Quo

The current ANM represents a typical half-year university course involving around 100 full-time graduate students from management-related subjects such as ISs, Management, or International Business and Economics. The course consists of weekly lectures and a negotiation journal. The journal is graded and provides half of the final grade. The other half comes from the end-of-course exam. ANM is designed to afford a total of 180 hours of work per student and semester. Teaching is supported using the VLE ILIAS (Graf and List 2005) to share learning material, upload and evaluate assignments, and facilitate communication between students as well as with teachers. Learning tools are completely pre-defined, requiring assignments to be turned in as Microsoft Office documents prescribing a minimum word count. Besides the official bulletin board and e-mail for questions and answers, other communication channels are not actively supported.

The ANM lecture covers face-to-face and electronic negotiations in a holistic manner, beginning with basic definitions and characteristics, then outlining the negotiation process. Preparation, execution, and evaluation of negotiations are taught applying them to electronic negotiations focusing on communication, decision-making and mediation aspects. Finally, selected topics from negotiation research (e.g. intercultural aspects) are discussed. The lecture involves numerous interactive individual and group tasks to enable students to experience negotiation aspects first-hand. For example, to illustrate negotiator profiling, students have to judge their fellow learners without talking to each other and report about their interests. To experience different negotiation styles (Kilmann and Thomas 1992), students engage in negotiation role plays with each other portraying specific styles, eventually evaluating each other's performance. Besides these interactive elements performed during lectures, the negotiation journal complements teaching providing several assignments to be completed outside the lecture to facilitate practical experience and reflection. All of these assignments have to be handed in in textual form or as a presentation for grading as well as feedback. The first assignment is a summary of individual expectations regarding the course and previous negotiation experience. Later on, students have to make requests in real-life contexts to experience and analyse when a person is not willing to fulfil a request and thus not willing to enter into a negotiation. The major assignment is to engage in an electronic negotiation simulation with fellow students or practitioners conforming to a predefined case study lasting from one to two weeks. This includes preparation, execution, and evaluation of this negotiation and of the negotiation partner, thereby applying the knowledge learned. Specific aspects of ex-post negotiation analysis are also practiced analysing negotiation scenes in movies (Kunkel et al. 2006).

Table 10 assigns the learning methods described above to their respective learning objectives according to Bloom's taxonomy. Although there is no real separation between passive lecture and interactive lecture as both are intertwined, they represent different methods leading to different objectives. While the passive part of the lecture focuses on lower order thinking skills regarding negotiation knowledge using slides and readings presented by the teacher for explanations, the interactive parts, including discussions, role plays, and case studies focus on higher order thinking skills e.g. by portraying specific negotiation styles in role plays. The assignments of the negotiation journal especially focus on higher order thinking skills and conceptual negotiation knowledge (e.g. evaluating methods for negotiation analysis applying them to movie scenes) as well as procedural negotiation knowledge (e.g. adoption of a negotiation process model in the negotiation simulation) being intertwined with the interactive lecture. Metacognitive knowledge is not explicitly addressed in the course, as it is very much prescribed by the teacher.

Table 10   Status Quo of Learning Methods According to Learning Objectives

The Knowledge Dimension	The Cognitive Process					
	Remember	Understand	Apply	Analyse	Evaluate	Create
Factual Knowledge	Passive Lecture (Explanations)	Passive Lecture (Explanations)	Interactive Lecture (Q&A)			
Conceptual Knowledge	Passive Lecture (Explanations)	Passive Lecture (Explanations)	Interactive Lecture (Role Plays, Case Studies)		Journal (Expectations, Requests)	
Procedural Knowledge	Passive Lecture (Explanations)	Passive Lecture (Explanations)	Journal (Movie Analysis, Simulation)			
Metacognitive Knowledge	Not Addressed					

3.4.3 Advanced Negotiation Management: Introducing the Personalised Learning Framework

Implementing the PLF to ANM means:

1) facilitating the construction of COI to enable learning in groups, providing an open climate (cf. components of Figure 14), and
2) supporting self-regulated personalisation following cognitive fit regarding learning tasks and tools (cf. relationships in Figure 14).

The learning method of the flipped classrooms neither facilitates personalisation per se, nor is it the only learning method being able to support self-regulated personalisation, however, it matches the learning objectives of ANM as well as provides enough openness for the PLF combining passive and interactive parts (Bishop and Verleger 2013). Therefore, we decided to follow the four-step cyclic model of the flipped classroom by Oeste et al. (2014) which is iteratively processed. One example iteration of this process will be described in the following to show how the PLF can be implemented. The negotiation journal runs in parallel to the online and co-presence sessions, providing more complex assignments following a self-regulated approach at the same time fostering diversity of tasks and tools compared to the status quo. Thus, PLEs can be introduced to a large scale, providing benefits such as collaborative self-regulated exploration and easy access to authentic tasks facilitating higher order thinking skills, consequently transforming journal entries to public blogs or wikis combining videos, images, or podcasts commented and assessed by peers and teachers.

In the first step (Objectives), an outline of the course is provided defining learning objectives and constraints regarding learning tasks, tools and collaboration. In the online learning phase, access to a course-related knowledge base is provided, containing learning units, videos, and readings to acquire basic factual and conceptual knowledge about negotiation basics, definitions, and seminal theories e.g. regarding negotiation process models and underlying phases (Adair and Brett 2005). The negotiation journal complements the iterations of the flipped classroom providing practical assignments. Similar to the status quo of ANM, a negotiation simulation can be used to illustrate the negotiation process, however, being executed in groups in a larger context requiring exploration of important concepts beforehand and evaluation afterwards. The focus of step one is to organise the learning process negotiating deconstruction of learning objectives into tasks and tools. Therefore, the learning groups have to gather knowledge regarding the relevant topics (i.e. negotiation basics) as well as regarding the learning process (i.e. learning tools in the domain of negotiations) referring to experiences and the knowledge base (i.e. internal and external representation of the learning domain/tool in Figure 15) to achieve a cognitive fit.

In step two (Exploration), students engage in learning gathering knowledge in a self-regulated, authentic way. For example, to achieve the learning objective of being able to conduct electronic negotiations, students gather information (e.g. on characteristics of electronic communication media relevant for negotiations) on the Internet, in papers, or in books. Conforming to the PLF, students are free to choose learning tools (e.g. mind maps or wikis) to paraphrase and rearrange relevant concepts. Training materials and access to NSSs is provided, including it in the PLE, to get the students familiar with such a system and prepare possible negotiation scenarios. As part of the negotiation journal, the simulation is conducted during this step. Conducting an electronic negotiation conforming to a case study, the students can apply, analyse and evaluate their knowledge acquired in the previous steps. A first form of re-evaluation and assessment is conducted within the learning groups aiming to achieve a satisfying result for all members. Further reflection will be encouraged as the student groups have to keep an electronic diary about the negotiation facilitating evaluation and creation of knowledge. Such a blog entry could link video clips to textual explanations of the negotiation process. Again, the students are able to choose for example the mode of representation using different social media tools increasing ownership and control, which consequently benefits satisfaction and learning outcomes. The focus of step two however, is on the management of these tools during execution of the learning tasks.

Step three (Evaluation) represents the first face-to-face session focusing on the interactive discussion of the previous steps to clarify and consolidate knowledge acquisition. Student groups present their negotiation diaries to each other and discuss their negotiation with their partnering groups. Students thus can present their expert knowledge regarding their individual learning objectives and their fulfilment, spreading this knowledge and thereby educating their peers, while the teacher moderates this process. Additionally, the learning process should be evaluated, providing assessments of the tool selection, management and achievement of learning outcomes to the peers.

Finally, step four (Immersion) focuses on the immersion of the knowledge acquired, employing further interactive presence learning by working with peer instruction, role plays, case studies, and readings exercised and discussed in class. Peer instruction (Mazur 1997) aims to deepen knowledge acquisition by posing realistic questions to the students integrating several of the learnt concepts. These questions can be answered anonymously via electronic voting systems or traditional methods requiring students to persuade their peers of their answer. Thus, peer instruction supports the integration of knowledge learnt in the self-regulated parts of the flipped classroom avoiding to embarrass students who opted for a wrong answer.

The concept of the flipped classroom presents a learning method, which fits the requirements of the PLF. Table 10 shows how the learning objectives of ANM can be addressed with implementing these methods as described above making them comparable to the current approach (cf. Table 11). The online parts of the flipped classroom (Objectives and Exploration) improve the passive lecture focusing on lower order thinking skills, the co-presence parts replace the interactive lecture focusing on higher order thinking skills, they are much more intertwined with the negotiation journal integrating higher order thinking skills in early phases. In total, the focus on the negotiation journal is increased fostering its self-regulated and collaborative character. In contrast to the current approach, metacognitive knowledge is now explicitly addressed communicating objectives in the beginning to scaffold the students choosing tasks and tools and facilitating peer assessment during the evaluation.

Table 11 Learning Methods according to Learning Objectives applying the PLF

The Knowledge Dimension	The Cognitive Process					
	Remember	Understand	Apply	Analyse	Evaluate	Create
Factual Knowledge	Flipped Classroom (Objectives & Exploration & Evaluation)					
Conceptual Knowledge	Flipped Classroom (Exploration & Immersion)				Self-Regulated Journal (Exploration)	
Procedural Knowledge	Flipped Classroom (Exploration & Immersion)		Self-Regulated Journal (Exploration/Simulation)			
Metacognitive Knowledge	Self-Regulated Journal (Objectives, Evaluation)					

3.5   Discussion

The following section compares the status quo of ANM with its modified version applying the PLF. Advantages and disadvantages of the framework are discussed from a learner's perspective as well as from a teacher's perspective also integrating external influence factors guiding the implementation of self-regulated personalisation in university courses.

The main advantage of the PLF is that it enables the learners themselves to personalise their learning experience in a self-regulated way. By handing over the responsibility for personalisation to the learner (who is then able to deconstruct learning objectives into tasks and tools), teacher-driven personalisation using learning styles becomes obsolete. Results of previous studies on learning styles and personalisation show its relevance; however, individual learning styles are too coarse a measure to define reliable matches between learning styles and learning methods (Gupta and Anson 2014; Melzer and Schoop 2014b). Personalisation is thus not imposed by the teacher anymore, but by the learners being scaffolded by the teacher. Furthermore, the PLF can be used as an alternative way to enable personalised learning and to explain its underlying relationships, deriving possible support capabilities regarding the personalisation of learning tasks and learning tools.

Self-regulated personalisation also improves the alignment of tasks within a course towards a central theme, which plays a pivotal role for learner satisfaction (Chan et al. 2014). However, the self-regulated alignment requires additional effort in negotiating tasks and tools in the learning group before engaging in the learning itself. In these negotiations, network effects (Shapiro and Varian 1999) play a vital role reducing the number of possible tools considerably, often inhibiting cognitive fit. Such a negotiation, however, is part of the learning process itself enforcing digital literacy and facilitating personal development (Hirshon 2005).

Collaborative, self-regulated learning heavily shifts responsibilities from the teacher to the learners providing ownership and control (Buchem et al. 2011) requiring extensive scaffolding (Tsai et al. 2013). Pedagogy in self-regulated courses must enable learners to make informed educational decisions providing metacognitive knowledge such as learning awareness and digital literacy. At the same time, open learning environments must be created encouraging application of diverse skills and knowledge with learner-centred forms of feedback and assessment (Green et al. 2005). As a consequence, self-regulated courses shift the focus towards learning processes instead of learning outcomes (Azevedo et al. 2008). Clear instructions, timely feedback, and competent staff – being relevant factors for learners' satisfaction according to Chan et al. (2014) – are thus particularly important in such personalised learning scenarios. Personalised learning is usually only implemented in rather small courses. ANM exhibits a considerable number of participants usually leading to anonymity and limited pedagogical opportunities for collaboration and interaction, which might decrease learning outcomes and satisfaction (Lehmann and Söllner 2014). However, personalised learning has been shown to counter these effects (Alonso et al. 2009), albeit requiring a suitable pedagogical integration, which is provided by the PLF. An integration as described in the previous section enables large numbers of learners to engage in real and practical exercises exploring the topic of negotiations in contemporary examples making the future value of the course easily recognisable for the learners (Chan et al. 2014).

There are also detrimental factors which must be considered planning and conducting self-regulated personalised learning. Besides the alignment of learning objectives within a course, the alignment of learning objectives and effort within a study programme is also important to the learners. Attending traditional courses and collaborative courses at the same time can be problematic as the latter require more effort distributed over the semester, while the former are mainly laborious at the end of the semester preparing for the exams. Increasing the number of collaborative and self-regulated courses in curricula may lead to a large-scale shift in the distribution of work. Seen from a staff perspective, the change in learning methods means a huge one-off effort developing and implementing a new course. At the same time, teaching becomes more efficient with the teacher being able to reuse learning units and videos for several classes and also using lecture time more efficiently focusing on interactive learning (Garrison and Vaughan 2011). However, teachers need to be comfortable handing over responsibilities to the learners. From a technological perspective, the teachers also need to be open and proficient to work together with learners using different software. Also, successful online learning material exhibits high quality, which requires a large amount of time to create and support. Matters of data security and copyright regarding such media on public platforms also have to be dealt with.

3.6   Conclusion

The evaluation by thought experiment to demonstrate feasibility presents the main limitation of this work. Regarding the literature, numerous concepts used in the PLF such as e-learning (Andersson et al. 2009), blended learning (Garrison and Vaughan 2011), flipped classrooms (Strayer 2012), and self-regulated learning (Azevedo et al. 2008) have proven their beneficial effects. However, the combination of all of these heterogeneous ideas has to be evaluated again analysing their interplay. Thus, our next steps will be to extend and implement ANM applying the PLF based on the thought experiment above. This instantiation of the course will then be evaluated combining design science research in ISs (Hevner et al. 2004) with DBR in the learning sciences (Brown 1992) aiming for a naturalistic ex-post evaluation focusing on quality, utility, and efficacy. Both methodologies require building and evaluating artefacts aiming to emphasise the connection between research rigour and practical relevance (Collins et al. 2004; Gregor and Hevner 2013).

From a theoretical point of view, the PLF is aimed to be generalisable to a broad range of courses and contents in IS education. However, it is very much nested into the constructivist learning theories. Thus, besides pursuing a practical evaluation, the framework should be applied to other courses varying content, learning methods or method of evaluation to improve its generalisability.

Finally, the definition of the PLF implies several directions for future research. Firstly, the PLF proposes a cognitive fit between learning preferences and tasks or tools as well as a task-technology fit between tasks and tools. The relationship between those processes needs further investigation. Also, such a cognitive fit is not always possible in learning groups with different preferences making analyses on group level necessary analysing the detrimental effects of missing fit. Secondly, the framework proposes two interdependent processes of cognitive fit, namely personalisation of tasks and personalisation of tools. Both processes are interdependent and are thus integrated into an overall cognitive fit for personalised learning. Whilst achieving cognitive fit reduces complexity and thus increases learning performance, the process of integrating both separate processes of personalisation might lead to interferences that increase complexity and thus decrease learning outcomes (Shaft and Vessey 2006).

4 Personalising the IS Classroom – Insights on Course Design and Implementation

Abstract
Personalising learning is one major avenue to address the increasing heterogeneity in today's (higher) education institutions. The present study discusses the design and implementation of a self-regulated, personalised flipped classroom course within the IS curriculum of a German university. Following a DBR methodology, relevant kernel theories are identified to derive general requirements and components for such courses, eventually describing the process of creating and implementing an instantiation transforming an existing university course. The requirements are evaluated referring to the implemented course, showing that e-learning reduces the effort of personalising the learning process.

Co-Author
Prof. Mareike Schoop, PhD

Re-publication of this article is performed with permission of the Association of Information Systems. The original article has been published in: Proceedings of the European Conference on Information Systems (ECIS) 2017, Personalising the IS Classroom – Insights on Course Design and Implementation, 2017, IS Teaching and Learning, Philipp Melzer, Mareike Schoop, available at http://aisel.aisnet.org/ecis2017_rp/90/

4.1   Introduction

From the Age of Enlightenment with scholars such as Wilhelm von Humboldt describing education as a moral imperative and personal responsibility (Berglar 1970) until today where education is often seen as an economic resource which must be maximised, individuals and societies have constantly striven to improve education. Today, more individuals than ever before receive extensive education, often provided by society. However, in a globalised world, learners pose increasingly heterogeneous requirements towards education, emanating from different goals, educational backgrounds, cultures, skills, and abilities (McLoughlin and Lee 2010).

Personalised learning is considered to be one of the major opportunities to improve education adapting learning processes to individual preferences regarding pace, methods, and contents (U.S. Department of Education 2010). As a result, there are currently numerous endeavours investigating and implementing personalised learning in research and practice (Pane et al. 2015; European Commission 2014). The two major avenues to achieve personalised learning are

1) self-regulated personalisation where the students are in charge of personalising their learning supported by the teacher and
2) adaptive learning where machine learning algorithms are used to analyse the learner's data to provide personalisation.

Both personalisation approaches are closely entangled with the digitalisation of learning processes, requiring e-learning support. In recent years, e-learning has become more than the mere substitution of traditional learning methods using electronic media. On the contrary, e-learning is augmenting, modifying, and redefining education creating new approaches, methods, and even paradigms (Puentedura 2003). One of these new learning methods is the flipped or inverted classroom aiming to switch

"events that have traditionally taken place inside the classroom now [to] take place outside the classroom and vice versa" (Lage, Platt, and Treglia 2000, p. 32).

With an increasing digitalisation of education, the idea of the flipped classroom has become the means of choice to implement self-regulated personalisation (Feldstein and Hill 2016; Bishop and Verleger 2013). However, there is still a considerable gap between the theoretical ideas of the flipped classroom and their practical implementation. Concepts and guidelines must be developed that adapt the flipped classroom to different educational institutions, subjects, and technologies. Besides only a small number of fundamental studies proposing beneficial effects of the flipped classroom, empirical results on learning outcomes, satisfaction, etc. are even more scarce (Findlay-Thompson and Mombourquette 2014).

The present study addresses this research gap aiming to improve teaching quality by building, implementing, and evaluating a course as part of the ISs and business curriculum of the University of Hohenheim as a self-regulated, personalised flipped classroom. The graduate course ANM is taught in the winter term of 2016 covering theories, concepts, methods, applications, and evaluation of business negotiations. The main feature of the transformed course is its implementation of personalisation on the level of learning tasks and learning tools using the PLF by Melzer and Schoop (2015).

After discussing our theoretical background (section 4.2), a short description of our research methodology (section 4.3) is provided. Following a design-oriented methodology, the paper focuses on the design of the course, deriving general requirements from the scientific literature and transforming these into general course components (section 4.4). These components are implemented in a real-life course, which is described in greater detail as a proof-of-concept to demonstrate its feasibility (section 4.5). Section 4.6 complements the practical description of the course showing how the requirements have been implemented sharing first key results gathered in the interaction with students. Finally, section 4.7 concludes the paper by summarising the approach and by discussing future research directions.

4.2 Theoretical Background

The proliferation of the social-constructionist learning paradigm (Kafai 2006) induced a large-scale shift of the responsibility from teachers to learners. According to constructivism, there is no transmission of knowledge from the teacher to the learner; instead, the learners construct their knowledge themselves based on experience, reflection, and discussion with teachers or peers. Teachers merely act as moderators in this process, guiding and supporting the learners. This paradigm-shift, which penetrates education from nursery to university today, paved the way for self-regulated learning putting the learners in charge. We analyse personalised learning on the level of learning tasks using Bloom's taxonomy for learning, teaching, and assessment (Anderson and Krathwohl 2001). It defines learning goals as a combination of cognitive processes (i.e. remember, understand, apply, analyse, evaluate, create) and types of knowledge (i.e. factual, conceptual, procedural, meta-cognitive). Furthermore, the taxonomy assigns specific learning tasks to each cognitive process (i.e. the process of understanding can be performed by the tasks of interpreting, exemplifying, classifying, summarising, inferring, comparing, explaining, etc.). Cognitive processes respectively learning tasks and knowledge types can be combined to create exercises or assessments such as "Explain relevant tasks within the negotiation preparation phase". These learning tasks and their resulting exercises are the basis of self-regulated personalisation, as each learner should be able to select tasks based on their individual preferences, requiring a set of different tasks available to achieve one specific learning goal. Supporting learning electronically, these learning tasks can be performed using specific e-learning tools. Bloom's taxonomy is not limited to face-to-face learning but has been extended towards electronic learning defining a wide range of learning tools supporting each learning task (Churches 2009; Bower, Hedberg, and Kuswara 2010).

Such tools might be provided in two different forms: Firstly, VLEs (often termed Learning Management Systems) – the most commonly used e-learning applications – are software applications which provide a common platform for teachers and learners for the creation, communication and administration of learning materials (Schulmeister 2003). However, they scarcely address self-regulated learning. Although such systems are used at almost every higher education institution today, only a small fraction of their features is actually used in practice (Gayer and Müller 2015; Meiers 2012). Self-regulated personalisation thus remains a task for the lecturers developing the didactic foundations of their courses. Secondly, a more recent approach to support self-regulated personalised learning electronically is the concept of PLEs. In contrast to a VLE, a PLE is no single software application but rather a set of hardware and software tools, often social media applications, used for learning, selected by the learner according to individual preferences (Attwell 2007). Whilst early definitions of PLEs mainly focus on third party tools, recent definitions see PLEs comprising of tools that may be provided by the learning institution and/or third parties (Kiy and Lucke 2016). Thus, a PLE may still be used after graduation for learning in the work place or even for informal learning at home.

To combine the ideas of self-regulated personalisation and PLEs, we use the PLF (Melzer and Schoop 2015; cf. Figure 16). The centre of the PLF encompasses lecturers and learners organised according to the COI framework (Garrison and Arbaugh 2007). Its overall goal is to provide a basis for designing and evaluating online and blended learning following a social-constructionist approach. The COI defines

1) social presence focusing on creating a sense of community be-tween the learners,
2) cognitive presence i.e. implementing learning using the practical inquiry model ultimately facilitating critical thinking, and
3) teaching presence i.e. designing and organising the course provid-ing instruction and facilitating discourse.

Within the PLF, the COI aims to personalise learning selecting learn-ing tasks as well as learning tools within a PLE that fit the learners' needs. This might require individual decisions, group negotiations, recommenda-tions, and/or prescriptions by the lecturer as processes of cognitive fit (Ves-sey 1991). Selected tasks and tools should fit in order to optimise learning as a process of task-technology fit (Goodhue and Thompson 1995). How-ever, there are several moderating factors influencing the process of per-sonalisation. The learning institution might influence personalisation by its strategy facilitating or sanctioning specific behaviour by its members. Also, the institution's infrastructure is an important factor. For example, there must be sufficient open learning spaces, computers, or access to a broad range of learning tools. Finally, the institution's learning culture must allow and support the freedom to personalise tasks and tools. The context of the learners also influences personalisation regarding

1) personal goals represented via the learning motivation (students with a high motivation certainly follow a different approach to reach their goals in studying compared to students with a lower motiva-tion and

2) personal context such as having to look after family members or having a job besides studying limits the resources left for studying and thus influence personalisation.

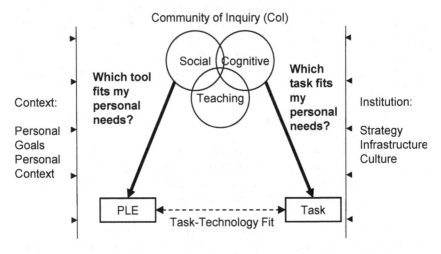

Figure 16   Personalised Learning Framework (Melzer and Schoop 2015, p. 7)

The most prominent method to employ self-regulated, personalised learning is the flipped classroom (Feldstein and Hill 2016; Bishop and Verleger 2013). Conforming to the notion of flipping the events from inside the classroom to outside the classroom and vice versa, a flipped classroom usually consists of two phases. The first is a distant phase, where the students acquire theoretical knowledge following explicit instructions from the lecturer supported by e-learning tools. The second is a presence phase – formerly the lecture – especially focussing on student-centred learning employing discussions and other interactive teaching techniques (Bishop and Verleger 2013). The flipped classroom implements a blended learning approach combining distance and presence education in a meaningful way. Its key feature is that in the lecture, lecturer and learners can rely on the previously acquired knowledge of the distant learning phase and focus on more sophisticated topics, application and immersion of the acquired knowledge. The distant learning phase is usually supported by videos or readings focusing on lower order thinking skills, while the presence learning phase focuses on higher order thinking skills such as applying, analysing, and evaluating the knowledge acquired.

The flipped classroom concept has been developed for school education. However, published studies on flipped classroom implementation mostly focus on higher education (Bishop and Verleger 2013). The flipped classroom has been proposed to foster active and collaborative learning in large classes, courses with a high amount of procedural knowledge and a large variety in learning tasks (Milman 2012; Pierce and Fox 2012). Although the flipped classroom is a trending topic in research and practice, scientific articles describing the design of a flipped classroom for a specific context or investigating its empirical effects on learning outcomes, satisfaction, grades, etc. are still scarce (Findlay-Thompson and Mombourquette 2014).

4.3 Methodology

The present study follows the pragmatist methodology of DBR which is prevalent in ISs research (Hevner et al. 2004) as well as in the learning sciences (Collins 1992). It aims to build and evaluate a practical instantiation of a self-regulated, personalised flipped classroom gaining exploratory insight into the numerous social, psychological, and technological factors influencing such a course. The paper at hand explicitly focuses on the design of the course describing

1) an explanatory design theory, deriving kernel theories from the literature to formulate general requirements which are then translated into general components and
2) a design method leading to a concrete instantiation of the course which will be evaluated (Baskerville and Pries-Heje 2010).

To identify kernel theories for the explanatory design theory, we performed a literature review on the topics of self-regulated and self-directed personalisation and the flipped or inverted classroom focusing on recent studies being published within the last five years. These kernel theories were mainly used to derive the general requirements which led to the design of the flipped classroom. Additionally, we thoroughly investigated the status quo of the course to be transformed performing interviews with the lecturer and post-doctoral research assistant that have taught the course for several years. The course contents have been identified and structured according to their respective goals, teaching methods, learning tasks, tools, and relative importance. This information was used as the basis for restructuring the course keeping the contents constant and at the same time adhering to the general requirements, components and didactic goals of a flipped classroom.

4.4   Explanatory Design Theory

In the following, we will derive requirements from the kernel theories (i.e. the PLF and COI), which are relevant conditions or capabilities to be fulfilled by a self-regulated, personalised flipped classroom. Table 12 lists those requirements in groups according to the related theoretical basis.

4.4.1   General Requirements

Personalisation is a concept that is not unique to the domain of learning. ISs deals with personalisation aspects, especially within the context of e-commerce, for several decades, e.g. in online shops to increase the specificity of service delivery for increased customer satisfaction. Personalisation research in IS defines three dimensions of personalisation, which we will apply to the domain of learning (Riemer 2002). The first dimension is the personalisation of products, services, and offers referring to the learning tasks and tools embedded into the flipped classroom. Such learning tasks and tools should be selectable and configurable by the learners themselves based on recommendations by the lecturer or a recommender software; tasks and tools should be open for combination across learning units (R1). The second dimension is the personalisation of websites requiring one central platform for learning whose content, features, layout, and navigation can be configured according to the individual preferences of the learner (R2). The third dimension is the personalisation of communication content, channels, and attributes referring to individual communication with each learner according to their individual preferences (R3). Additionally, such personalisation must be supported by the lecturer providing the freedom and guidance necessary for the learners e.g. to be able to select and configure learning tasks and tools (R4; Melzer and Schoop 2015).

Further requirements emerge from institutional and contextual factors described in the PLF. Irrespective of whether VLEs or PLEs are used to implement a flipped classroom, we require learning tasks and learning tools to be provided via one central platform, often the VLE or course-website that the institution provides (R5). This ensures that necessary infrastructure and management support for implementing a flipped classroom are provided including computer and learning facilities, which are irreplaceable in blended learning. It also ensures that lecturers and learners are familiar with the learning platform which increases its adoption. Especially ease of use of such systems has been deemed to be an important role (Parker and Herrington 2015; Melzer and Schoop 2014b; Miller 2012). Online learning is nevertheless still higher effort for the learners, as they must learn to use new technologies as well as new contents at the same time. Therefore, extensive support must be provided to the learners, e.g. through institutional trainings or specific course tutorials to learn how to use the necessary technologies (R6).

Further requirements are derived from the COI framework's social, cognitive, and teaching presences (Garrison and Arbaugh 2007). Achieving social presence and a sense of community requires open and affective communication between the learners directly face-to-face or in electronically mediated channels (R7). However, to achieve group cohesion, such communication must be directed towards an intellectual focus representing the course's learning goals. Therefore, collaboration needs to be encouraged either providing opportunities to learn in groups or even including collaborative tasks as mandatory course elements (R8). To foster cognitive presence, the model of practical inquiry should be used for learning defining four steps (Garrison and Arbaugh 2007):

1) triggering an event (i.e. identifying a problem for further inquiry);
2) exploration (i.e. investigating the issue through reflection and discourse);
3) integration (i.e. synthesising the ideas generated through exploration); and
4) resolution (i.e. applying the knowledge to other contexts).

The flipped classroom mirrors practical inquiry in several aspects. On the one hand, identifying a specific problem to tackle is especially important in distant learning phases since there is only limited communication between lecturer and learners (Bishop and Verleger 2013). On the other hand, reflective learning activities are in the focus (Miller 2012). Practical inquiry eventually fosters critical thinking; to fulfil this goal, especially practical and collaborative learning tasks are necessary (R9; Garrison and Arbaugh 2007). Teaching presence leads to three separate requirements. The lecturer is responsible for designing and organising the course i.e. managing the interplay of social and cognitive presence through employing specific learning methods and technologies and adjusting them during instruction. This also includes keeping the overall effort of a flipped classroom comparable to a normal course and providing online learning within small chunks to ensure motivation (R10; Miller 2012). Teaching presence also encompasses facilitating discourse between the learners online as well as in presence learning to establish and maintain the community and at the same time keeping this discourse content-centred. Online forums, for example, have been found to show more interaction the higher the number and quality of lecturer posts (R11). Besides that, it requires direct instruction jolting and maintaining cycles of practical inquiry making sure to achieve the learning goals (R12; Garrison and Arbaugh 2007).

There are further requirements specific to the course at hand. They will be discussed in section 4.5.

Table 12   List of Requirements for Self-Regulated, Personalised Flipped Classrooms

#	Group	Description	Kernel theories
R1	Personalisation of tasks and tools	Provide personalisation of products and services	(Melzer and Schoop 2015; Riemer 2002)
R2		Provide personalisation of websites	
R3		Provide personalisation of communication	
R4		Provide freedom and guidance for personalisation	
R5	Institutional and contextual factors	Provide a central platform for learning	

R6		Provide reasonable IT infrastructure & support for learners	
R7	COI: social presence	Enable open communication	(Garrison and Arbaugh 2007)
R8		Encourage collaboration	
R9	COI: cognitive presence	Enable practical inquiry	
R10	COI: teaching presence	Design & organisation	
R11		Facilitate discourse	
R12		Direct instruction	

4.4.2   General Components

In the following, we will derive seven general components from these requirements, which eventually form the basis for creating a flipped classroom. A blended learning course design always has to balance three heavily intertwined dimensions namely didactics, content, and technology. We structure our components according to these dimensions also addressing their overlaps.

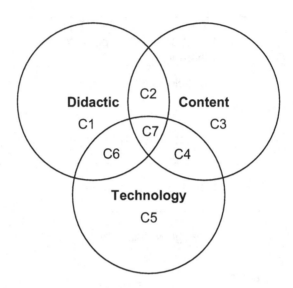

Figure 17   Didactic, Content, and Technology Dimensions and Related General Components

The didactic concept of the course needs to implement the core ideas of the flipped classroom providing a distant learning phase as well as a presence learning phase. However, these phases need to be structured in greater detail defining exactly when to provide opportunities for personalisation, collaboration, inquiry, instruction, and discourse (C1). Such a structure is usually provided by the lecturer, but is equally important for learners, especially in complex blended learning scenarios (Garrison and Vaughan 2011). Combining experiences from the model of practical inquiry (Garrison 2011) and the flipped classroom process model (Oeste et al. 2014) we define three phases:

1) a distant preparation phase focusing on the self-regulated acquisition of theoretical knowledge;
2) a presence lecture focusing on reviewing the preparation and immersing into more advanced questions using interactive teaching methods; and
3) a distant reflection phase enabling extensive individual reflection on the acquired knowledge.

Creating a real course requires the transformation of abstract learning methods into real exercises, which are to be performed by the learners reflecting the course's learning goals. Both collaborative learning and practical inquiry require learning tasks reflecting higher order thinking skills such as application, analysis, evaluation, or creation of knowledge. At the same time, performing such cognitive processes facilitates discourse between the learners. Along with common guidelines on creating learning materials, cognitive processes (Anderson and Krathwohl 2001) and corresponding learning tasks can be used to formulate exercises. In contrast to other flipped classroom approaches which implement distant learning mainly to acquire knowledge (i.e. lower order thinking skills), we aim to include higher order learning tasks throughout the course supporting our three-phase model of the flipped classroom. Each iteration of these three phases represents one course unit (C2). Figure 18 shows our personalised flipped classroom process model and the learning methods and tools assigned to each phase. Whilst the first phases explicitly encourage students to learn in groups and even perform exercises in parallel eventually synthesising their knowledge, that every group member has the necessary knowledge before the lecture, the third phase aims towards individual reflection on expectations and learning outcomes. Students receive individual feedback for each portfolio entry.

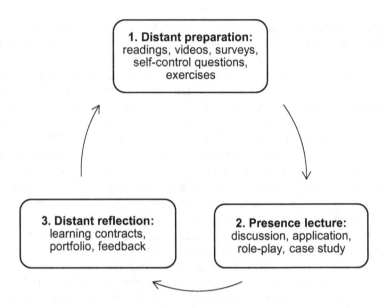

Figure 18   Personalised Flipped Classroom Process Model

The course content is also heavily intertwined with the didactic concept as well as the technology used to implement the course. As we aim to keep the contents constant to make the course comparable to previous years (C3), the only changes concern the new technologies to enable and support personalisation of products, services, websites and communication. While most learning tools already provide possibilities to personalise their user interface, a forum can be provided to enable personalised asynchronous communication for groups. Additionally, individual mail or personal communication within the VLE can be useful (C4).

Technological aspects of the flipped classroom are mostly implemented using a VLE as a central platform. Its institutional advantages (i.e. existing familiarity, trainings, IT infrastructure, and support) outweigh its disadvantages compared to PLEs (i.e. variety in tools, informal learning). Although this seems to be a controversial point for a course explicitly aiming to personalise learning, we argue that a VLE does not hinder self-regulated personalisation but can be used as a central platform to link to more personalised learning tools and thus provide a guided path towards personalisation. A VLE's main purpose is to facilitate design and organisation of learning courses. It, therefore, provides one source already offering most products and services and extensive manufacturer documentation and support as well as additional support and trainings at the institution (C5).

Since the technology employed should support the desired didactic methods, it is vital to increase digital literacy of the learners and at the same time provide the technology with a purpose reflecting the course's goals. Although, most learners today are so-called digital natives (Prensky 2001), acquiring new knowledge parallel to acquiring it in an electronic and therefore unfamiliar way requires high effort (McLoughlin and Lee 2010). Therefore, increased emphasis has to be put on informing learners about the organisational structure of the flipped classroom (C6).

Eventually, all components described above have to be balanced against each other creating a real-life university course (C7).

4.5   Practical Design Theory

4.5.1   Course Specifics of Advanced Negotiation Management

Following the discussion of general requirements and components in the previous chapter, we will now focus on the practical design of our self-regulated, personalised flipped classroom university course ANM. This discussion will also include four further requirements specific to the general topic of the course which is negotiation management and in particular on negotiation planning, implementation, media, technology, and evaluation (cf. Table 13). Negotiations are a topic that cannot be learned theoretically. Rather, a combination of theory and practice must be the basis (R13; Lewicki 1997). Switching from a traditional course to a flipped classroom inherently leads to a switch in the role of the lecturer from that of mainly a teacher to that of the expert guiding and supporting the learners (R14; Melzer and Schoop 2014c). Since flipped classroom concepts rely on a solid electronic learning base, the technological aspect is even more important than usual in negotiation teaching. Thus, both face-to-face and electronic negotiations should be considered (R15; Köszegi and Kersten 2003). Finally, the need for assessment is even greater in self-regulated learning. Thus, the assessment in a negotiation course must be continuous and in a formative and summative manner (R16; Milman 2012).

Table 13   Negotiation Specific Requirements

#	Group	Description	Kernel theories
R13	Negotiation Didactics	Teach negotiation theory and practice	(Melzer and Schoop 2014c; Lewicki 1997; Köszegi and Kersten 2003; Milman 2012)
R14		Include negotiation expert knowledge	
R15		Address face-to-face and electronic negotiation topics	
R16		Provide formative (and summative) assessment	

All requirements and components for self-regulated, personalised flipped classrooms can now be integrated as shown in Table 14.

Table 14   List of General Components for Self-Regulated, Personalised Flipped Classrooms

#	Group	Description	Requirements addressed
C1	Didactic	Use a process model to structure the course	R1, R8, R9, R10, R11, R12
C2	Didactic & Content	Focus on higher order thinking skills throughout the course	R8, R9, R11

C3	Content	Provide correct and comprehensive content	R13, R14, R15, R16
C4	Content & Technology	Provide content using suitable technologies	R1, R2 R3, R4
C5	Technology	Use one central platform	R1, R2, R3, R5, R6, R10, R11
C6	Technology & Didactic	Extend organisational & technical support for learners	R1, R4, R6, R7, R10, R12
C7	Didactic & Technology & Content	Balance didactics, technology and content	R1, R4, R7, R8, R9, R13, R14, R15, R16

ANM is attended by approximately 120 to 150 management and ISs graduate students. The course has been in place in its pre-flipped classroom form for several years as a weekly lecture course. Following the idea that negotiations have to be taught theoretically and practically, the lecture aims to transmit factual knowledge regarding seven chapters (i.e. negotiation basics, negotiation planning, communication aspects, decision and negotiation analytics, electronic negotiations, dispute resolution, and culture in negotiations) while at the same time providing numerous opportunities to apply this knowledge in a variety of practical learning tasks such as small role-plays and case studies. The lecture is accompanied by several assessments during the term in the form of negotiation journals written by the students (making up 50% of the final grade), representing their reflections on the course content and their practical applications. The final exam assesses a broad range of knowledge acquired posing a recent real-life negotiation case study to be analysed requiring lower as well as higher order thinking skills. It makes up the other 50% of the final grade.

4.5.2   Creating a Personalised Flipped Classroom from Advanced Negotiation Management

Although this course might not be the standard university course, providing a rather high degree of practical learning to a large number of students, we are convinced that it is destined to be transformed into a flipped classroom for further support of its variety of different learning tasks and self-regulated learning increasing the degree of personalised learning by sharpening its profile. To elicit the status quo, we conducted semi-structured interviews with the lecturer that created and taught the course since 2009 and the research assistant involved in the practical tasks. Using these interviews, we wanted to create a very fine-grained log as to which teaching methods are used corresponding to specific slides within each lecture, what learning goals they aim for, and how much lecture time they require. The resulting log then formed the basis for the restructuring of the course into a flipped classroom, mostly aiming to put theoretical teaching and corresponding topics into the preparation phase, while practical teaching methods and topics were kept in the lecture. At the same time the overall order of topics as well as the overall amount of effort for the students had to be kept within meaningful levels. This ultimately requires organisational decisions, e.g. when to begin with the first preparation phase, how many flipped class-room cycles to conduct, which material to discuss in the lectures, and how to activate the students in such a large course.

The new course was developed over several months with the general requirements and components in mind (cf. Tables 12 - 14). Regarding the practical implementation of our flipped classroom concept, one of the most important decisions was to use the open-source VLE ILIAS (German for "Integrated Learning, Information, and Work Cooperation System") as a central platform. ILIAS is one of the most frequently used VLEs at German universities with installations in 91 higher education institutions and the University of Hohenheim as one of them (ILIAS e.V. 2016). ILIAS provides numerous features in the areas of personalisation, learning and course management, cooperation, communication, assessment, and competence management. Its features are comparable to other VLEs such as Moodle as it can be used to provide all course elements relevant for the preparation (learning modules, questions, readings), lecture (file management), and reflection phase (e-portfolio and assignments) as well as lateral features such as communication facilities in a flipped classroom. However, the main contribution of this work is not about the choice or implementation of a VLE, but about its integration and extensive use of the available features to support self-regulated personalised learning in a flipped classroom.

4.5.3   Advanced Negotiation Management as a Personalised Flipped Classroom

Based on the interviews and on the existing course material, we created an ILIAS learning module as the basis for the preparation phase. It serves as a reader for the students comprising of several webpages structured according to the eleven course's units each representing one iteration of the flipped classroom process model. Each unit consists of several pages on instructions and learning goals, preparation content, and concluding remarks what to do next (e.g. writing an e-portfolio entry). Each unit begins with explicit instructions (e.g. "Perform an analysis of platforms for Electronic Conflict Management") and corresponding learning goals (e.g. "Being able to analyse Electronic Conflict Management platforms regarding communication media employed and conflicts targeted") stating what the learners need to do in order to prepare for the next lecture as well as describing the competencies necessary to follow this lecture. The description of learning goals directly refers to the exercises stated within the preparation pages and were created using Bloom's taxonomy. They represent the interface between preparation and lecture for lecturer and learners as both can check here, which competencies should have been acquired during preparation. The pages presenting the content for preparing the lecture are based on the slides, which were previously part of the lecture and their corresponding notes. However, considerable effort went into restructuring, extending, and enhancing these materials providing a sound basis for preparation. We achieved this by following the structure of learning tasks and learning goals. Self-regulated personalisation is supported by enriching the textual basis of the reader through alternative learning tasks varying according to Bloom's cognitive processes and learning tools (e.g. reading a paper versus watching a video versus answering a survey versus checking the acquired knowledge answering self-control questions on cognitive biases in decision-making) providing content in various multimedia formats. The students are most of the time free to decide which one of the learning tasks to address or how to divide the tasks within their learning groups.

The lecture phase at first glance represents a traditional lecture at a university. Differences emerge in the didactic practices employed. The lecturer uses material such as excerpts from negotiations for the students to apply their knowledge. Case studies and role plays are used to apply the knowledge and to combine different concepts from various chapters of the lecture. Fishbowl exercises allow selected students to show their negotiation skills in front of their colleagues who in turn can analyse, criticise, and advise their learning peers (e.g. portraying different negotiation styles). Finally, important factual knowledge is rephrased by students in their own words to check whether they have understood the contents in a deep way to be able to talk about it in their own words. Since learners are prepared, more emphasis can be placed on sophisticated topics, application, and immersion of these topics performing interactive teaching techniques such as critical thinking, role-play, case studies, discussions, surveys, and assessments (Galbraith 2004). For example, the students learn about the debate of the cues-filtered-in versus the cues-filtered-out approach in order to apply it to negotiations conducted via electronic communication media (Walther and Parks 2011). In previous years, the lecture focused on transmitting factual knowledge about each perspective. Since the students prepared this factual knowledge in the flipped classroom, they now discussed their individually preferred perspective in order to make them stand in for the opposing perspective and persuade their peers accordingly, leading to fierce discussions and critical thinking.

The reflection phase is structured using the teaching technique of learning contracts requiring the students to submit several e-portfolios over ILIAS (Galbraith 2004). It enables learners to write an individual blog directly in ILIAS in the form of a personal portfolio, which can be accessed and graded by the lecturers including individual feedback. Each learner writes down individual expectations and goals she wants to achieve during the course in the beginning enforcing the learners to self-regulate their learning increasing metacognition. At the end of the course, the contract is evaluated in another portfolio entry on lessons learned as to which learning goals have been fulfilled and which have not, inducing reflection on the learning process. As part of this framework of the learning contract, further content-related journal entries have to be written to reflect deeply on the course's content and learning. ANM includes a negotiation case study, which enables the learners to negotiate with other students to apply their knowledge acquired about negotiations. This negotiation is the subject of one of the portfolio entries facilitating reflection on preparation, implementation, and results of the negotiation from both participant's perspectives.

Through all phases, open communication between lecturer and learners needs to be facilitated. Therefore, an electronic forum within ILIAS is used moderated by the research assistant supporting the course. Furthermore, additional ILIAS personalisation features are used in the course. The system displays recommended timeframes when to perform which preparation units, lectures, or journal entries. Learners also have the possibility to track their individual learning progress in the course.

4.6   Evaluative Discussion

Having described in detail how requirements relate to components of a self-regulated, personalised flipped classroom (cf. section 4.5), we now describe how each requirement is implemented presenting the key results of our approach.

Personalisation of products and services (R1) has been enabled by stating alternative learning tasks which vary according to the cognitive processes and learning tasks of Bloom's taxonomy. Besides that, a variety of learning tools is offered. Students are encouraged to learn in groups whilst preparing the lectures as well as during the lectures (R8) and select the learning tasks and tools in a self-regulated way, eventually synthesising their results with the help of the lecturer. Regarding personalisation of websites (R2), we heavily rely on the features of the VLE ILIAS used in the course, providing the possibility to personalise its look and feel as well employing the communication facilities in the form of a forum and mailings together with personal communication and standard e-mail to communicate with the students reflecting their preference (R3). The freedom of selecting tasks and tools is supported by a 60-minute tutorial on individual learning styles employing a questionnaire at the beginning of the course. Furthermore, learning tasks as part of the distant preparation phase are clearly marked as individual or group tasks (R4). ILIAS as a central learning platform is employed (R5), heavily relying on the university's IT infrastructure and trainings. However, additional effort is exerted on creating and integrating additional tutorials into the online preparation and presence lectures (R6). Besides that, open communication is facilitated employing a forum as well as answering questions personally and via email as soon as possible (R7). Employing our adapted flipped classroom process model (cf. Figure 18), we implemented the process of practical inquiry (R9). Requirements on teaching presence have been implemented preparing the new course structure beforehand and maintaining it continuously during the lecture phase explicitly gathering feedback from the students to improve the course further (R10). The new course structure leads to far more sophisticated and lively discussion during the lecture (R11) integrated with elements of direct instruction (R12). Such an approach requires an expert lecturer, being capable of combining negotiation theory and practice (R13) including electronic negotiations (R15) as well as dealing with numerous different topics ad hoc (R14). Finally, besides the traditional summative assessment, numerous efforts have been exerted to provide formative assessment in the form of self-control questions after the preparation phases and the portfolio entries, summing up each unit (R16).

Albeit, a thorough evaluation of the transformed course is beyond the scope of this paper. First experiences gathered observing the course and interacting with the students are promising. First of all, personalised learning is often criticised for its increasing effort for the lecturers providing alternative tasks and tools. According to our experience, there was a considerable up-front effort to transform lecture slides and notes into the ILIAS learning module. However, during the semester, lecturer effort was almost comparable to traditional lectures, because a lot of questions by the students are answered automatically providing extensive e-learning contents online. Since ANM is the only flipped classroom course in their curriculum, the students needed some time at the beginning to adapt. After approximately three weeks of teaching, communication within the forum became very open and active (much more so than in previous years and in other traditional courses with a similar forum) with students posing and discussing questions to several course-related topics. Therefore, we agree with Lehmann et al. (2015) on the importance of interactivity in flipped classrooms. Furthermore, the students perceived the IT-infrastructure to be sufficient but requested even more course-specific and ILIAS-related tutorials, as many of them just started their graduate studies and were unfamiliar with the VLE ILIAS. We, therefore, extended our tutorials and created additional ones. Tutorials regarding learning methods were evaluated differently by the students. As graduate students most of them said, that they already knew how to learn. Therefore, demand was much higher for the technical tutorials. Our efforts to encourage the students to prepare and learn in groups remained largely unheard. Students reported that they did not form learning groups due to the fact, that they did not know their peers at the beginning of their graduate studies and did not trust them enough to synthesise different knowledge while preparing the lectures. Therefore, they rather prepared the lectures alone, accepting the additional effort. In general, students reported high time-effort for the course which led to a separation of the students into two groups. Over the course of the semester approximately half of the participating students evaluated the course as being worth the effort keeping on preparing and participating in the lecture. The other half of the students used the online materials to prepare for the exam avoiding the lectures and their inherent interactivity. Similar separations have already been described in flipped classrooms (McNally et al. 2017) as "flip-endorsers" and "flip-resisters". While not performing the preparation tasks does not lead to specific sanctions apart from lacking behind during the lecture, ILIAS statistics reveal that approximately three out of four students performed the preparation tasks. Creating a cohesive COI, therefore, did not work out for all students. Especially students who want to join the course several weeks after it started are hindered by entry barriers such as already existing learning groups, acquired knowledge of peers, and missed tutorials. From a lecturer's perspective, teaching in a flipped classroom atmosphere is demanding. For once, the lecturer needs to be prepared to answer any suggestions, questions, critiques the students think about. This is much more the case as the students spend extensive time preparing for the lecture. Furthermore, new material is required for applying, contrasting, and illustrating the factual knowledge to create deep knowledge that can be combined, explicated, and communicated. Comparing it with the previous course, it is obvious that the discussions and interactions in the flipped classroom are on a much higher intellectual level showing that the preparation (albeit gently forced) leads to effective results and lasting knowledge experiences requiring an expert lecturer.

Generalisability of the presented work is one of its main limitations. While the general requirements and components can be used to design further personalised flipped classroom courses, the presented design is specific to its environment, course topic, and implementation. Our flipped classroom is one of very few courses following this concept in the curriculum of the participating students. Therefore, they are used to traditional university teaching and needed some time in the beginning of the course to adapt and explore their new environment. To employ more flipped classroom courses a curriculum-wide perspective is necessary for their meaningful integration carefully planning the overall student-effort (Schaper and Tipold 2015). The transformed course followed a rather practically-oriented approach even in its previous form due to the subject. Therefore, workload for planning and implementing the practical lectures might have been lower compared to other courses. Another limitation of our study is that lecturer and advisor are at the same time researchers analysing the course.

4.7   Conclusion

The present paper describes the design of a self-regulated personalised flipped classroom university course presenting general requirements and resulting components derived from the PLF (Melzer and Schoop 2015). Following a DBR methodology requirements and components are implemented transforming the university course ANM at the University of Hohenheim into such a flipped classroom and implementing it. First experiences from designing and implementing the course show that personalising learning can be less effort for the lecturers than previously thought, if electronic learning tools are included. The course atmosphere was much more open and interactive than in traditional courses increasing satisfaction and learning for lecturers and learners. However, we experienced the learners to gradually separate into groups of "flip-endorsers" and "flip-resisters" (McNally et al. 2017) having less than half of the students attending the lectures at the end of the semester. In accordance with the literature, we experience that there is no one-size-fits-all approach incorporating personalised learning or the flipped classroom (Findlay-Thompson and Mombourquette 2014). Therefore, we agree with the literature and request the publication of further flipped classroom designs – providing blueprints for practitioners how to conduct a flipped classroom – and their evaluation aiming to disentangle the complex relationships between learning methods and learning outcomes.

5 Towards a Holistic Evaluation Concept for Personalised Learning in Flipped Classrooms

Abstract
Incorporating the student's preferences regarding pace, methods, and contents into teaching is particularly hard in today's higher education, providing courses to large numbers of students often over electronic media. Such personalised learning can be implemented via self-regulated learning approaches using the method of the flipped classroom. However, literature on the design and evaluation of such courses is scarce. Evaluation models and instruments are not adapted to the specific nature of the flipped classroom yet, combining presence and online teaching. The present paper aims at conceptualising a holistic approach towards an evaluation concept for personalised learning. Based on an overview of evaluation models in the learning sciences and ISs domains an evaluation concept is presented and applied to a course instantiation focusing on the topics of (1) fulfilment of general requirements and effects on (2) learning outcomes, (3) adoption, and (4) individual factors of the students.

Co-Author
Prof. Mareike Schoop, PhD

© Springer Fachmedien Wiesbaden GmbH, part of Springer Nature 2019
P. Melzer, *A Conceptual Framework for Personalised Learning*,
https://doi.org/10.1007/978-3-658-23095-1_5

5.1   Evaluating Modern Teaching and Learning

Universities have long held an unrivalled position in delivering higher education. Traditionally, lectures, example classes, tutorials, laboratories, and other forms of teaching were the formats of choice. What they all have in common is that they are lecturer-centred in that the lecturer directs the learning process, the forms of interaction (if any), the teaching method(s), and the learning directions and is thus the focal point of such courses.

Nowadays, it is an acknowledged fact that students have different needs and approaches of acquiring knowledge. Heterogeneous groups of students exhibit a large variety of individual factors (e.g. educational background, cultural background, personality traits, skills, and abilities), which require personalised teaching and learning. Personalised learning aims to incorporate individual preferences into the learning process regarding pace, methods, and contents (U.S. Department of Education 2010). This is not a new idea as it has been done by lecturers and students on a daily basis. However, especially in large classes and online learning environments, personal preferences of students are difficult for the lecturer to consider. New approaches towards personalised learning, therefore, follow the constructionist learning paradigm (Kafai 2006), putting the students in charge of their own learning process. One method to do so is self-regulated learning, which emphasises the students' metacognitive abilities (i.e. knowing about one's own learning). Self-regulated learning aims to empower students to plan, implement, and reflect their learning for continuous improvement. Thereby, students should be enabled to derive learning strategies matching their individual preferences overcoming previous limitations (Zimmerman 2002).

E-learning supports the ideas of personalised learning, providing learning materials at any place and any time. Especially blended learning as the combination of presence and electronic learning opens up new avenues of learning (Garrison and Vaughan 2011). One method to implement blended learning in a meaningful way is the flipped classroom. It combines not only presence and electronic learning but also self-regulated and lecturer-moderated (rather than lecturer-centred) learning. Flipped classrooms turn around traditional lecture and tutorial teaching, requiring a distant preparation phase performed by the students themselves, consequently enabling the lecturer to discuss and apply the acquired knowledge within the lecture (Lage et al. 2000). The distant preparation phase, therefore, relies on the integration of e-learning technology (Strayer 2012).

Whilst the idea of the flipped classroom seems to be very promising for improving active, collaborative, and self-regulated learning, scientific dissemination on concrete course design, evaluation, and learning outcomes is still scarce (McNally et al. 2017; Abeysekera and Dawson 2014; Butt 2014; Bishop and Verleger 2013; Pierce, Fox 2012). This is problematic because there are various ways to implement a flipped classroom course design depending on its topic, theory-focus, assessment-focus, full-flip or partial-flip, etc., which require a generalisable approach to evaluation (Bishop and Verleger 2013). Furthermore, the students have different preferences and requirements towards a flipped classroom, which must be incorporated (McNally et al. 2017). Evaluation instruments focus either on learning or on the use of e-learning tools, often neglecting their combination. Finally, learning interventions exert a plethora of psychological, social and technological effects regarding the students, lecturers, and institutions all being related to each other.

Therefore, the research goal of this paper is to develop an evaluation concept for personalised flipped classrooms and apply it theoretically to an example course to show its feasibility. The paper thus follows a design-oriented approach comprising of a build and evaluate cycle on the evaluation concept itself as an artefact (Hevner et al. 2004). Developing an evaluation concept, we specifically focus on scientific evaluation aiming towards understanding whether and how flipped classrooms work and what effects they exert, not teaching evaluation, which is conducted due to university quality assurance.

The paper is structured as follows. Section 5.2 presents the chosen design-oriented research methodology. The overview of existing evaluation models and instruments for learning interventions regarding their main constructs self-regulated learning, learning outcomes, adoption, and individual factors is explained in section 5.3. Section 5.4 describes the conceptual background of the personalised flipped classroom and its implementation in a real university course to which the evaluation concept will be applied to. Section 5.5 presents the resulting evaluation concept discussing methodological aspects as well as proposing a combination of the frameworks and instruments presented in section 5.3. Finally, section 5.6 summarises and discusses the presented evaluation concept showing future research directions.

5.2 Methodology

This study is part of a larger research project to analyse the effects of personalised learning in a holistic manner, following a design-oriented research methodology. Such a pragmatist approach is prevalent in ISs (Hevner et al. 2004) as well as in the learning sciences (Brown 1992; Collins 1992) striving to create knowledge by designing solutions to practical problems. The designed artefacts resemble complete real-life learning interventions or software, which are applied to their intended context. Thus, evaluation is not restricted to artificial scenarios but happens within a natural environment providing rich insights and continuous improvement (Anderson and Shattuck 2012). However, a design-oriented methodology is not restricted to solving a specific problem. In contrast, it aims to generalise findings beginning with instantiations of courses or software to mid-range theories eventually creating grand theories (Gregor and Hevner 2013).

In our previous work a personalised flipped classroom has been designed and implemented over a complete semester at a German university (Melzer and Schoop 2017a). The present paper aims to develop a sound evaluation concept for this course. However, the target of this evaluation is not only the instantiated course, but also its underlying PLF (Melzer and Schoop 2015) and the general requirements derived from it.

5.3 An Overview of Models and Instruments for the Evaluation of Personalised Learning

Bishop and Verleger (2013) distinguish three dimensions regarding the evaluation of flipped classrooms:

1) lecturer or student as object of analysis,
2) objective or subjective analysis, and
3) time and quantity of analyses.

To evaluate learning interventions from a student perspective investigating student engagement, Fredricks and McColskey (2012) name several measurement methods such as student self-report surveys, lecturer ratings of students, interviews, and observations. An evaluation of a learning intervention only from a student's perspective, however, would be incomplete as students cannot estimate, for example, the achievement of learning goals planned by a lecturer. Moreover, one could argue that the institution in which the learning takes place also affects the learning and therefore could be a viable object of analysis.

While objective measurement focuses on grades and scores in various forms (Findlay-Thompson and Mombourquette 2014), subjective measurement gathers perceptions and opinions from the participants. Objective measurement in the learning sciences is usually differentiated into formative and summative measurement. Formative scores encompass for example self-control tests employed before or during lectures to test, whether students are able to follow the course. Hence, summative scores are grades or points achieved in the final exam conducted after the semester. While the literature on flipped classrooms requests formative assessment to motivate the students to prepare as well as provide a constant measure of retention (Lehmann et al. 2015; Bishop and Verleger 2013; Milman 2012), McNally et al. (2017) specifically reports on the importance of summative measurements.

Finally, there are several research designs including matched or unmatched pre-post-test designs requiring a differing number of surveys or tests. Looking at the literature, it can be stated that there are very few approaches that actually implemented and reported on flipped classroom design and evaluation. The majority of the 24 studies found by Bishop and Verleger (2013) measures subjective student perceptions whilst only two investigate objective student performance (Day and Foley 2006; Moravec et al. 2010). Only one of the studies evaluates the flipped classroom over a complete semester (Day and Foley 2006). Furthermore, Bishop and Verleger (2013) find that only half of the studies employ matched pre-posttests whereas the other half employs post-tests only. In the following, we will therefore present theories and instruments which have been used in the domains of learning sciences and ISs to evaluate personalised learning interventions and are adaptable to flipped classrooms providing a holistic approach to evaluation.

5.3.1 Self-Regulated Learning

Self-regulated learning is seen as a way for students to address individual factors during the learning process (Zimmerman 2002). The student's awareness and knowledge about the learning process itself is seen as the key factor, which must be implemented appropriately. It includes tasks such as setting learning goals, deriving learning strategies, monitoring learning performance, restructuring physical or social context, time management, self-evaluation as well as understanding its results, and finally adapting the learning accordingly. Self-regulated learning is defined to be proactive and therefore matches the core idea of the flipped classroom. Furthermore, self-efficacy and self-motivation have been found to be important predictors of learning performance (Zimmerman 2002).

A comprehensive instrument which can be used to investigate self-regulated learning is the Motivated Strategies for Learning Survey (MSLQ) analysing a student's motivation as well as specific learning strategies as its main constructs (Duncan and McKeachie 2005). It is cited over 650 times (Google Scholar 2017) and generally reported to achieve valid results (Fredricks and McColskey 2012). The construct of learning motivation comprises of several factors, namely intrinsic and extrinsic goal orientation, task value, learning control, self-efficacy, and test anxiety. Learning strategies represent general skills such as organisation, metacognition, time management, as well as specific strategies such as rehearsal, critical thinking, peer learning, and help seeking. While the MSLQ assesses self-regulated learning in traditional learning interventions, Liaw and Huang (2013) analyse predictors of self-regulated learning in e-learning environments. Although they state a comprehensive model of self-regulated learning in e-learning environments as a remaining research challenge, they show that self-regulation depends on the interactive learning environment, satisfaction, and usefulness of the environment and individual factors such as anxiety and self-efficacy. Nevertheless, self-regulated learning usually focuses on constructs from the learning sciences, ignoring an ISs perspective.

5.3.2   Learning Outcomes

Learning Outcomes are best reflected by analysing formative or summative student grades or scores as objective measures focusing on a learning intervention as a whole. As a subjective measure, perceived quality of the teaching can be used to show the success of a learning intervention.

Therefore, the Information Systems Success Model (ISSM; DeLone and McLean 1992; DeLone and McLean 2003) has been adapted to the domain of e-learning measuring information quality (i.e. accuracy, completeness, ease of understanding, and relevance of the materials), system quality (i.e. availability, ease of use, reliability, and response time), and service quality (i.e. overall support) of online courses (Chiu et al. 2007).

These constructs reflect antecedent factors of IS success, comprising of intention to use, actual use, user satisfaction, and net benefits. The ISSM, adapted to e-learning, however, is one of the very few instruments combining constructs focusing on learning itself as well as technological factors.

5.3.3 Adoption

Adoption of ISs is widely investigated using the Technology Acceptance Model (TAM; Venkatesh and Bala 2008), which poses perceived usefulness and perceived ease of use as key predictors influencing the behavioural intention to use a software as well as the usage behaviour.

TAM has already been adopted in the research area of e-learning showing the importance of perceived usefulness and ease of use in this domain. Furthermore, highlighting the importance of multimedia system functionalities, system interactivity, critical mass, computer self-efficacy, subjective norm, and content quality as additional predictors of system use (Gross et al. 2016; Sung Youl Park 2009; Pituch and Lee 2006; Lee 2006; Selim 2003). Furthermore, several studies have shown that actual usage of an e-learning tool and user satisfaction are related to each other (Sun et al. 2008; Liaw and Huang 2013).

5.3.4 Individual Factors

Individual factors are also investigated within the learning sciences as well as ISs. Such factors can be related to demographic variables such as gender, age, or job status (Lu and Chiou 2010), personal context, or institutional factors (Melzer, Schoop 2015). Self-regulated learning, for example, relies very much on the personality traits of task anxiety, self-efficacy, and learning motivation (Duncan and McKeachie 2005).

Personality traits also reflect individual factors, which have been thoroughly investigated in the domain of personalised learning as learning styles (Coffield et al. 2004) and ISs as cognitive styles (Robey and Taggart 1981). Both streams of research, however, provide inconclusive findings (Scott 2010 and Huber 1983). Thus, we acknowledge weak effects of individual factors, being relevant to categorise the types of students and their reaction towards flipped classrooms. Individual factors have been found to affect different e-learning constructs such as learning outcomes (Melzer and Schoop 2016) and satisfaction (Lu and Chiou 2010). Furthermore, individual preferences have been used as categorisation measures grouping students in a flipped classroom into flip endorsers and flip resisters explaining their behaviour (McNally et al. 2017).

5.4 A Personalised Flipped Classroom University Course

The following section explains the theoretical underpinnings of a personalised flipped classroom in the form of general requirements. Moreover, a concrete university course which serves as the basis for our evaluation concept is described.

5.4.1   The Personalised Learning Framework

Following the notion of the PLF (Melzer and Schoop 2015), we understand personalised learning as an inherently active and collaborative process. The PLF combines the COI framework (Garrison 2011) with the theory of Cognitive Fit (Vessey 1991) to explain personalised learning in blended learning environments (cf. Figure 19). The COI framework conceptualises a social, cognitive, and teaching presence. While social presence requires creating and maintaining cohesive learning groups, cognitive presence models the individual learning following the process of practical inquiry. Teaching presence eventually models design and implementation of classes, scaffolding, and facilitating discourse between students. The COI is able to personalise learning in electronic contexts following the idea of Cognitive Fit selecting learning tasks and tools according to their personal or group preferences. This, however, requires the availability of alternative tasks and tools to achieve the desired learning goals. While learning tasks can be defined according to Bloom's Taxonomy of Learning (Bloom et al. 1984; Anderson and Krathwohl 2001) into lower (remember, understand, apply) and higher (analyse, evaluate, create) order thinking skills, learning tools are defined using the notion of PLEs. PLEs are defined as a wide variety of electronic tools that facilitate learning including operating systems, office applications, as well as social media tools (Attwell 2007). The process of personalisation is affected by several contextual and institutional moderators, namely the university's strategy, infrastructure, culture, and the student's personal goals and context.

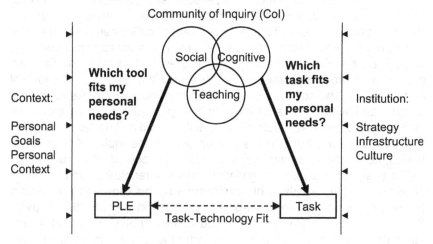

Figure 19   Personalised Learning Framework (Melzer and Schoop 2015, p. 7)

From the PLF, Melzer and Schoop (2015) derive several general requirements for personalised flipped classrooms. Firstly, personalisation must be provided. Personalisation concerns learning tasks (e.g. exercises) and tools (e.g. websites, social media tools) and communication facilities. Consequently, the lecturer must provide freedom and guidance for personalisation on a central learning platform supporting the students with reasonable IT infrastructure and support (Melzer and Schoop 2015). A VLE can be used as a central platform with links to other websites, tools, or services similar to a PLE. Establishing social presence requires open communication between participants and encouraging collaboration while cognitive presence is implemented by the model of practical inquiry facilitating an exploration-based approach to learning. Teaching presence requires the lecturer to design and organise the course, facilitate discourse, and provide direct instruction where necessary (Garrison and Arbaugh 2007).

5.4.2 From a Traditional Lecture to a Personalised Flipped Classroom

The course to be transformed into a personalised flipped classroom is associated to a business and ISs curriculum of several master programmes including about 120 to 150 students per year at a German university. The course is recommended for attendance in the first semester and comprises weekly lectures, five negotiation journal entries, and a final exam. The final grade comes from the exam result (50%) and the grades on the journal entries (50%). The course is taught in English focusing on planning, conducting, and evaluating negotiations in business contexts using traditional face-to-face as well as electronic negotiation media. The lecture aims to provide knowledge from an ISs perspective on the topics of negotiation basics, negotiation planning, communication aspects, decision and negotiation analytics, electronic negotiations, dispute resolution, and culture in negotiations. It leaves plenty of time for applying this knowledge in practical tasks such as discussions, role-plays, and case studies. Further application and reflection tasks are performed in the negotiation journal, where students have to negotiate in real-life with other people, analyse negotiations as well as assess their own negotiation behaviour.

For the winter term of 2016, this course has been transformed into a personalised flipped classroom (Melzer and Schoop 2017a). Combining and adapting existing approaches from self-regulated learning (Zimmerman 2002) and flipped classrooms (Oeste et al. 2014; Bishop and Verleger 2013), the course is organised in three phases:

1) preparation (i.e. self-regulated preparation of theoretical knowledge in groups performing personalisable learning tasks over personalisable learning tools);
2) lecture (i.e. the lecturer focuses on student-centred discussions and guides applications of the previously learned knowledge to broaden and deepen the knowledge acquisition);
3) reflection (i.e. individual reflection on preparation and lecture performing sophisticated learning tasks writing the negotiation journal over an online course).

This process model is implemented using the VLE ILIAS (ILIAS e.V. 2016) as a central platform for preparation, communication, materials, and reflection. Personalisation is thus implemented providing alternative learning tasks and tools to achieve learning goals within the preparation (e.g. read a paper vs. watch a video to understand a topic) as well as within lectures (e.g. discuss vs. perform a role-play to apply a topic) and reflection (e.g. through broad task descriptions and multimedia support facilitating reflection). Students are encouraged to prepare in groups according to their individual preferences and synthesise the acquired knowledge before respectively in the lecture.

5.5   An Evaluation Concept for Personalised Learning in Flipped Classrooms

The following section presents the developed evaluation concept for personalised learning. Starting with its methodological underpinnings, the previously presented evaluation models are arranged to fit personalised learning in flipped classrooms.

5.5.1   Methodology

The main goal of the present work is to design a general evaluation concept for personalised learning, which will be applied to the personalised flipped classroom described in section 5.4. Its first step should thus be to check whether the general requirements derived from the PLF have been implemented correctly and are noticed by the students. Furthermore, learning outcomes, adoption, and individual factors have to be assessed. Figure 20 displays relevant constructs as well as their relationships. These constructs will be assessed using a mixed-method approach as suggested for the holistic evaluation of learning interventions by the design-oriented methodology (Anderson and Shattuck 2012) as well as previous studies on flipped classroom evaluation (Fredricks and McColskey 2012; McNally et al. 2017).

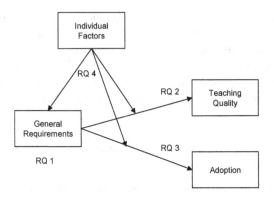

Figure 20   Underlying Constructs for the Evaluation of Personalised Flipped Classrooms

Figure 21 summarises the presented evaluation concept incorporating qualitative and quantitative analysis of subjective perceptions and quantitative analysis of objective performance of the students and the corresponding measures. The quantitative survey on subjective student perceptions and objective performance is complemented by qualitative data gathered using journal entries, interviews, and observations. Therefore, rich insights can be obtained refining and extending the previously identified constructs (Venkatesh et al. 2013).

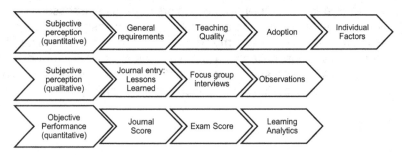

Figure 21   Subjective and Objective Evaluation Measures

5.5.2   Application of Measures

Subjective perception regarding our constructs of interest is measured using a post-test survey. First of all, it investigates whether the general requirements regarding the flipped classroom course have been fulfilled, namely personalisation of tasks and tools, inclusion of institutional and contextual factors as well as implementation of the COI framework involving social, cognitive, and teaching presence. Regarding the requirements of personalisation, new survey items have to be created. Additionally, the MSLQ instrument is used to assess, whether self-regulated learning occurs during the course as a precursor for personalisation at the same time assessing learning strategies (Duncan and McKeachie 2005). To investigate the social, cognitive, and teaching presences defined in the COI framework, we employ the corresponding pre-validated COI instrument (Arbaugh et al. 2008). This instrument has been used in several studies, which evaluated online and blended learning courses employing the COI framework (Lambert and Fisher 2013; Shea and Bidjerano 2010) and is able to indicate the quality of the social, cognitive, and teaching presences as well as their relationships.

Secondly, learning outcomes are evaluated following the ISSM (DeLone and McLean 2003) adapted to the e-learning context focusing on information quality, system quality, service quality (Chiu et al. 2007) and satisfaction (Liaw and Huang 2013).

Adoption – especially of the course's online parts – is investigated using the TAM constructs perceived ease of use, perceived usefulness, perceived self-efficacy, and perceived anxiety (Venkatesh and Bala 2008). These constructs – together with perceived satisfaction and interactive learning – are of particular relevance since they have been found to be predictors for the level of self-regulatedness of an e-learning environment (Liaw and Huang 2013).

As individual factors, we operationalise demographics, contextual and institutional factors (Melzer and Schoop 2015), and learning styles (Honey and Mumford 1992).

Regarding the qualitative analysis, semi-structured focus group interviews with volunteering students are conducted to investigate important factors that emerged in the survey and clarify or complement the findings. The aim is to have three focus groups with at least four students each mixing the courses of study and the individual factors to achieve sufficient heterogeneity within the focus groups facilitating discussion (McLafferty 2004). To encompass not only the student perspective but also the lecturer perspective, observational notes are documented by the lecturer and the supporting research assistant observing the presence lectures. These notes focus on their experiences teaching the course and providing online and offline clarifications, explanations, and content support regarding all of the course topics.

Objective performance of the students is evaluated analysing the negotiation journal entries (which represent the end of each flipped classroom cycle) showing the final learning outcomes. Thus, scores of these journal entries can be used to estimate learning outcomes within the corresponding units. Furthermore, scores of the summative exam written at the end of the semester can be analysed representing ultimate learning outcomes. Usually, single exam tasks correspond to specific units or topics covered in the course. Therefore, exercise scores can be analysed to investigate learning outcomes of specific units. However, these objective performance indicators have to be handled with care, since there is no valid direct comparison possible due to the change in teaching methods and in the student sample at the same time. Nevertheless, they can be analysed with reference to the respective course units focusing on specific topics, learning tasks, and learning tools.

Finally, measures provided by the learning analytics features of the VLE ILIAS are investigated. Although, ILIAS only provides limited data, forum and mailing statistics can be used to complement the measures on personalisation of communication (i.e. which communication media are used?), social presence and group cohesion (i.e. how many posts are written per medium compared to other courses), and adoption (i.e. access data or ratings of specific preparation pages, learning tasks, and learning tools).

5.6   Discussion and Outlook

This present paper reports on a holistic, mixed-method evaluation concept for personalised flipped classroom university courses following a design-oriented methodology. The described personalised flipped classroom is grounded in the PLF. Due to its novelty and the scarce literature on similar approaches (McNally et al. 2017; Abeysekera and Dawson 2014), a holistic evaluation concept is required combining models from the learning sciences and ISs. In particular, the evaluation concept elicits whether

1) the theoretical requirements regarding personalisation have been fulfilled from a student perspective,
2) the learning outcomes have been improved,

3) the adoption of e-learning elements has been successful, and
4) individual factors acting as moderators can be explicated.

Compared to the scarce literature on flipped classroom creation and evaluation, our concept is unique in several ways. Firstly, it provides a holistic perspective on flipped classroom evaluations and personalised learning following the PLF employing quantitative and qualitative methods. Furthermore, it incorporates all relevant factors present in a real-life university course to create a comprehensive picture.

The presented approach, however, also has some limitations, which mainly stem from its design-oriented approach. Since we want to evaluate a real-life university course over a complete semester providing real grades, it would be unethical and even more effort to instantiate a control group that would receive different teaching. Due to the one-semester character of the implemented flipped classroom, knowledge is gained during the semester. A pre-post-test design investigating learning outcomes would therefore be self-fulfilling and has been discarded. Finally, there are numerous variables that have been identified for investigation of our constructs leading to a high number of constructs for our survey. Therefore, we decided to split the survey into several parts assessing different constructs and topics at different points in time during the course to keep the participant's effort small. Stable constructs such as individual factors are assessed in the beginning of the course, while fulfilment of general requirements, learning outcomes, and adoption are assessed at the end. An evaluation after the exam, when the students have performed the complete course, would not be meaningful either, since the time-span between the last lecture and the exam is usually several weeks. Impressions would have been faded out too much. Furthermore, the proposed interviews may be subject to bias involving volunteering students. Following the results of McNally et al. (2017) there are different groups of students including flip endorsers and flip resisters. Students volunteering for an interview before the final exam probably are mostly flip endorsers.

The quantitative evaluation is partly redundant to the standard student evaluation of teaching prescribed by the university for quality assurance. However, both surveys are necessary, since the student evaluation of teaching does only partly address our constructs of interest (e.g. assessing the quality and adoption of e-learning, self-regulated personalisation, or individual factors). With regard to section 5.3, we only found very few instruments capable of addressing learning interventions comprising of presence and online learning. Instruments rather investigate either presence or online learning not being able to analyse their interrelationships. Furthermore, the question remains whether exam grades are a truly objective measure of learning outcomes. On the one hand, the lecturers are the ones grading the exam and creating the evaluation standards. On the other hand, a qualitative analysis of graded journal entries might not reveal the students' true opinion, since some might focus on what they think the lecturer wants to read to achieve more points. Besides the lecturing effort, also the efforts to employ the abovementioned holistic evaluation concept is rather high. Although many studies analysing flipped classrooms or learning in general incorporate mixed-method approaches (e.g. comprising of a survey and interviews Lambert and Fisher 2013) the majority focuses on single survey post-test analyses (Bishop and Verleger 2013). Thus, an ex-post analysis of the value of each evaluation method has to be performed refining the presented approach by extending, omitting, or altering specific methods. Overall, we do indeed provide a novel evaluation approach as we have provided a novel teaching approach, both calling for further research in the field of personalised learning.

6 Discussion and Outlook

While the previous chapters reflect the two-staged approach of this thesis

1) to identify influence factors of and
2) develop support for personalised learning,

the following discussion aims to summarise and evaluate this thesis' findings with regard to similar research and derive its major contributions.

6.1 Discussion

Beginning with an investigation of the status quo of personalised learning, this thesis replenishes the theories of learning styles (Honey and Mumford 1992) matching practical and theoretical learning styles to enactive and vicarious training methods. If such a matching is achieved in negotiation trainings, better skill acquisition and application of the knowledge learned is proposed leading to more effective, efficient, and fairer negotiation outcomes. These assumptions are tested in a laboratory experiment assigning the participants to negotiation trainings conducted using distinct training methods. While personalised learning – indicated by matching learning style and training method – leads to positive effects on the acquisition of electronic negotiation skills, as well as the efficiency and fairness of negotiation outcomes, the effects of the training method are found to be much stronger.

Dwelling on these results, learning tasks (i.e. the tasks learners perform according to a specific training method) are decided to be the main object of analysis. Creating a generalisable framework of personalised blended learning (i.e. the PLF) the learners are modelled as a self-regulated COI (Garrison 2011). Based on Bloom's taxonomy of learning tasks (Bloom et al. 1984; Krathwohl 2002) and taxonomies of social media learning tools (Churches 2009; Bower et al. 2010), the learners personalise their learning selecting and using learning tasks and learning tools according to their individual respectively group preferences. This process of personalisation is explained using cognitive fit (Vessey 1991). A learning task must fit the mental representation of a learning task-solution, while a learning task supported by a learning tool must fit the mental representation of the learning tool-solution. Furthermore, learning task and learning tool have to be compatible following the notion of task-technology fit (Goodhue and

© Springer Fachmedien Wiesbaden GmbH, part of Springer Nature 2019
P. Melzer, *A Conceptual Framework for Personalised Learning*,
https://doi.org/10.1007/978-3-658-23095-1_6

Thompson 1995). If such a fit can be achieved, learning performance will increase. Besides this process of personalisation, institutional and contextual variables are of major importance influencing the personalisation of learning tasks and learning tools (Gross et al. 2016; Ganzert et al. 2017).

Building on the PLF, a design and implementation for the course Advanced Negotiation Management (ANM) at the University of Hohenheim is created to show the feasibility of the approach. Developing an explanatory design theory, twelve general requirements are derived from the PLF namely: the personalisation of

1) tasks and tools,
2) website, and
3) communication;
4) freedom and guidance for personalisation;
5) a central platform for learning backed by
6) reasonable infrastructure and support for the users,
7) open communication and
8) collaboration between teacher and learners,
9) practical inquiry as a training method, and a teacher who is responsible for
10) course design and organisation,
11) facilitating discourse, and
12) direct instruction.

While these requirements must be present in any kind of self-regulated personalised learning course, further negotiation-specific general requirements are:

13) teaching negotiation theory and practice,
14) including negotiation experts,
15) addressing face-to-face and e-negotiations, as well as
16) formative and summative assessment.

These requirements are translated into seven general course components, which must be present in any course aiming to personalise learning. They can be structured by balancing didactics (i.e. using a flipped classroom process model, focusing on higher order thinking skills throughout), content (i.e. providing correct and comprehensive content using suitable tools), and technology (i.e. using one VLE extended by sufficient organisational and technical support for its users). Besides the explanatory design theory, a practical design theory is presented, showing the implementation of a proof-of-concept design of the ANM course, which aims to personalise learning using the method of the flipped classroom (Strayer 2012).

This design and implementation show numerous avenues to operationalise self-regulated personalised learning leading to different course designs at the same time requiring different evaluation concepts. Therefore, a holistic evaluation concept is developed by Melzer and Schoop (2017b) encompassing models and measures from the learning sciences as well as ISs research. Furthermore, following a design-oriented research methodology, mixed-method approaches are often suggested combining the strengths of quantitative and qualitative measurement to achieve a comprehensive picture of the numerous variables involved in a real university course (Anderson and Shattuck 2012; Bishop and Verleger 2013). The proposed evaluation concept focuses on the achievement of the postulated requirements, learning outcomes, adoption, and individual differences.

6.1.1   A Comparison to Recent Work in the Field

The following integrative discussion aims to evaluate the results presented in the previous chapters. Thus, their different foci and research methods are synthesised providing a holistic perspective on influence factors, design, and support potentials for personalised learning. The findings are embedded into related literature.

Modelling personalised learning, learning styles are probably the most prominent measures in the scientific literature. As a comparison, Google Scholar provides 3.780.000 resulting articles regarding learning styles, while personalised learning only leads to 75.700 articles (Google Scholar 2017). Furthermore, learning style theories and instruments, as measures which are easy to understand and apply, are marketed in non-scientific publications and consulting (Honey and Mumford 2000; Kolb and Kolb 2005) and therefore are very influential in policy making, corporate education, and schools. A poll among teachers in Great Britain and the Netherlands revealed that 85% of the participating teachers believed in learning styles and 66% of them used learning styles in their schools (Weale 2017). Furthermore, there is also a broad corpus of scientific literature advocating the use of learning styles for personalising learning admitting positive effects towards numerous variables (cf. Chen and Chiou 2014; Kumar et al.

2011). While the literature supports that learners have individual differences regarding the presentation of knowledge, evidence regarding positive effects of a matching between these learning styles and the mode of instruction is questioned in the scientific literature (Dekker et al. 2012; Scott 2010; Pashler et al. 2009). Literature reviews on learning styles find over 70 different models and instruments often having conflicting underlying assumptions (Cassidy 2004; Coffield et al. 2004). Coffield et al. (2004) analyse the 13 most influential models still finding no consistent picture. Furthermore, evidence that the developed theories and instruments are valid supporting the matching hypothesis is weak (Pashler et al. 2009). This is in line with the results presented in chapter 2, confirming a significant effect of a matching on skill acquisition, however indicating a considerably stronger effect of the training method on learning outcomes. Although individual differences of the learners are at the centre of personalised learning, learning styles alone are an insufficient measure. The PLF is therefore based on observable learning tasks. Such tasks directly relate to the training methods as a subset of the didactic concept laid out by the teacher. Furthermore, the PLF puts emphasis on the context of the learner defining several moderating influence factors.

The theoretical basis of the PLF needs to be discussed as well, as it combines cognitivist and constructionist approaches, which might appear to contradict each other at first. Cognitivist psychology investigates the transmission and processing of information in the brain leading to learning effects (Woolfolk 2014). Cognitive approaches analyse individual differences in information processing, e.g. cognitive processes (Bloom et al. 1984), cognitive load (Sweller 1988), cognitive fit (Vessey 1991), or task-technology fit (TTF) (Goodhue and Thompson 1995) in learning and decision-making. Later cognitivist theories also take into account groups of individuals better reflecting collaborative learning in SCT (Bandura 1977; Bandura 1989). The constructivist learning paradigm and especially constructionism, however, neglect a knowledge transfer between teacher and learner, proposing that knowledge is constructed by the learners themselves. Constructionist approaches are based on practical, collaborative, and situated learning (Kafai 2006) building on late social cognitivist theory. While the basis of the PLF – Bloom's taxonomy of cognitive processes – is rooted in a cognitivist perspective on learning, it is applied in the PLF within a model of learning, which is embracing the constructionist learning paradigm. The original taxonomy (Bloom et al. 1984) has been extended and transformed to recent learning tasks (Anderson and Krathwohl 2001; Krathwohl 2002) and learning tools in its revised version (Churches 2009; Bower et al. 2010) to encompass a constructivist perspective. Cognitive load theory was applied to learning processes defining course design principles to minimise cognitive load (van Merrienboer and Sweller 2010). The flipped classroom was also able to minimise cognitive load (Abeysekera and Dawson 2014). To the best of my knowledge, this thesis provides the first contribution combining cognitive fit and personalised learning. Furthermore, the PLF models two interdependent processes of cognitive fit, personalising learning tasks and learning tools at the same time. Such interdependent processes have been modelled within the domain of software development (Shaft and Vessey 2006). However, they introduce further complexity bearing the possibility of interference between both processes of personalisation leading to delays and therefore decreased learning outcomes. Finally, the PLF incorporates also a task-technology fit component. TTF has been analysed in the context of e-learning showing positive effects on the impact of a VLE in case of perceived fit (McGill and Klobas 2009; McGill and Hobbs 2008). Such fit is moderated through the learning purpose and the learning process (Sun and Wang 2014).

For the evaluation of the PLF, a real-life personalised flipped classroom course is designed and implemented. To generalise the chosen approach, this course instantiation is compared to the increasing literature on flipped classroom course designs regarding

1) content,
2) learning methods, and
3) operationalisation.

Flipped classrooms are developed in all academic fields and for varying contents, however, course designs are particularly disseminated in the domains of medical education, pharmaceutical education (McNally et al. 2017; McLaughlin et al. 2014; Pierce and Fox 2012), and management education (Findlay-Thompson and Mombourquette 2014; Butt 2014) including ISs (Lehmann et al. 2015). Accreditation councils request active learning approaches in higher education (Pierce and Fox 2012) and at the same time increasing numbers of students require an efficient approach to teaching (Lehmann et al. 2015). All of the aforementioned flipped classroom designs are targeted towards undergraduate students, confirming the results of the literature review by Bishop and Verleger (2013), while the approach presented in this thesis is one of few designs explicitly focusing on graduate students.

While other course designs see personalisation as a side-effect of the flipped-classroom, the one described in this thesis is the only one particularly focusing on personalised learning employing learning methods and techniques accordingly. This results in a higher level of interactivity and collaboration within the distant preparation phase compared to other course designs. Most designs include pre-recorded lecture videos as means of instruction (Bishop and Verleger 2013; Pierce and Fox 2012), however, including interactive elements to facilitate application of the knowledge, self-control of the learning, and collaboration to a varying degree. A course design similar to the one presented in this thesis by Lambert and Fisher (2013) describing a flipped classroom design implemented in a course focusing completely on distant learning, includes many more active and collaborative tasks such as blog entries, wikiing, and video conferences among the graduate learners. Other courses range from an equal distribution of theory and application (Lehmann et al. 2015) down to 20% complex concepts and application and 80% theory (McLaughlin et al. 2014).

When designing a personalised flipped classroom according to the PLF, the context of the students is very important. Regarding the operationalisation of such flipped classrooms mandatory preparation phases increase entry barriers for students who are joining a course late, since their peers already acquired large amounts of knowledge. Furthermore, it is important to motivate the students to prepare before the lectures (Miller 2012). The literature usually focuses on intrinsic motivation showing the benefits of thorough preparation, requiring, and extending the prepared knowledge in the lecture. However, the importance of formative assessment during the semester is highlighted in the literature motivating the students extrinsically (Bishop and Verleger 2013). Empowering the learners to personalise their learning by selecting different learning tasks and learning tools requires profound metacognition (Zimmerman 2002; Miller 2012) as well as sufficient digital literacy (Lehmann et al. 2015). Those might be less developed in a course involving undergraduate students. With graduate students, however, there are effects of habituation to previous traditional learning experiences and other traditional courses within their curriculum. If students are used to traditional lectures and learning at the end of the semester, they might be completely overwhelmed by the contents of the preparation phase. In addition, they might not understand that the lecture extends the preparation tasks taking it for a mere substitution for the lecture. Therefore, explicit instructions on the organisation and goals of the flipped classrooms organisation are vital. Furthermore, implementing a flipped classroom requires extensive infrastructure regarding a VLE and respective tutorials of the learners. Therefore, personalised flipped classroom designs are bound to higher education, where all those requirements are met.

6.1.2 Limitations

Design-oriented research originated from the contrast between controlled laboratory experiments and the analysis of real-life learning in situated scenarios (Brown 1992; Hevner et al. 2004). Although DBR aims to achieve the best of both worlds, conflicting underlying assumptions of the methodology lead to several limitations of this thesis.

DBR (Collins 1992) requests teachers as co-investigators, who formulate relevant requirements, as well as a broad range of expertise in different areas addressing the numerous variables involved in learning. However, it also requests an objective evaluation differentiating between the designers of a learning intervention and those who evaluate and test it. The present approach only partly differentiates between designer, teacher, and researcher. In chapter 2, the designer of the trainings also held the trainings and evaluated them in the end, however, being supported by the lecturer of the ANM course. In the design process described in chapter 4, the design was mainly informed by the PLF and the designer was assisting the lecturing of the course ANM, albeit also developing the final evaluation.

DBR requests systematic variation within sites (Collins 1992). Chapter 2 provides such variation investigating different treatment groups in a laboratory experiment having a manipulation as well as a control group. Nevertheless, such a systematic variation can hardly be maintained if a complete university course is modified and implemented due to ethical reasons. Therefore, investigating the ANM course in chapter 4, students were not informed about research interests regarding the course and respective modifications in order to prevent biases. However, there were no treatments providing systematic variation only to previous instantiations of the

ANM course taught in the past. However, comparisons have to be performed with caution. While course contents, lecturers, or curricula might be the same, the course participants have changed.

Finally, DBR as well as design science research request multiple iterative evaluations (Collins 1992; Hevner et al. 2004). While this thesis provides the design of a personalised flipped classroom course as a first evaluation of the PLF, proposing a general evaluation concept for further evaluation, more iterative improvement and evaluation is required.

Although the PLF is meant to be a framework leading to generalisable requirements and components for courses implementing personalised learning, the present analyses are conducted only within the domain of negotiation teaching. Negotiation teaching is identified as a domain, which especially facilitates the acquisition of practical and theoretical knowledge. However, the PLF needs to be applied to other courses teaching different topics. An even greater step towards generalisability would be to transfer the PLF from higher education to schools or professional trainings. Such a transfer, however, is questionable, as the PLF is particularly based on research regarding higher education and the implemented course showed that it matches the requirements of graduate students very well. A third dimension, which requires a transfer of the PLF, is culture. Defined as an institutional context factor in the framework itself, the PLF originated in Western higher education culture being implemented in the German system. However, other learning cultures, university cultures, or national cultures might address self-regulated personalisation differently. From a lecturer's perspective, the German system significantly differs from the Anglo-American system of higher education and research regarding freedom of research, course load, and funding (Eymann et al. 2014). From a learner's perspective, differences emanate from national culture. Eastern cultures for example have been found to put higher value on educational outcomes such as degrees and grades, they focus more on rote learning and avoid conflicts and confrontation if they disagree to the knowledge provided by the lecturer (Bing and Ping 2008; Boondao et al. 2008). Moreover, learning and teaching in different cultures also vastly differ regarding the course size (Schoop and Booth 2016).

6.1.3   Contribution

The major contributions of this thesis are described in the following, focusing on

1) learning tasks as the unit of analysis of personalised learning,
2) cognitive fit as a theory to analyse personalised learning,
3) general requirements and components for the design of personalised flipped classroom courses, and
4) evaluation criteria and instruments for such courses.

While the first two topics resemble the key contributions of the PLF (cf. chapter 2 and 3), the latter two topics result from the proof of concept course design, implementation, and evaluation concept (cf. chapters 4 and 5).

Having discussed the limitations of learning styles as instruments to personalise learning, this thesis uses learning tasks actually performed by the learners as the basis for personalisation. This grounds personalised learning on observable actions instead of conflicting learning style theories. Whilst context, describing different learning strategies, learning motivations, learning cultures, and even learning paradigms, is reflected in learning style theories, it is also driving them apart and therefore making a general application of these theories impossible. The PLF suggests to provide alternative learning tasks and learning tools as well as to let the learners select and use them according to their individual or group preferences. The presented lists of learning tasks and learning tools are non-exhaustive examples, which need to be extended. However, they show a practical method for personalising learning, which can be performed by teachers and lecturers incorporating the motivation and responsibility of the learners themselves. An evaluation of the developed proof-of-concept course ANM from the perspective of the students' shows that they embrace the responsibility, interactive teaching, and metacognitive knowledge acquired (Krieg et al. 2017). Discussing different learning style theories can even be used as a didactic method to create awareness for individual learning preferences with the students.

The application of the theories of cognitive fit and task-technology fit provide a sound theoretical basis for such self-regulated personalised learning. Having been already applied to individual styles in decision-making, they provide a stepping stone for the scientific investigation of self-regulated personalised learning. Cognitive fit enables the formulation of relationships between mental processes of learning, the selection and use of task and tools, and resulting learning performance. Task-technology fit requesting that learning task and learning tool have to be compatible complements the PLF.

Another major contribution of this work is the design of a personalised flipped classroom course combining the PLF and the learning method of the flipped classroom. By employing the flipped classroom method, the benefits of blended learning approaches can be leveraged making personalised learning possible in an effective and efficient way. Blended learning facilitates several aspects of personalisation such as increased availability and repeatability of the learning materials. Criticism regarding personalised learning is often uttered because of the parallel provisioning of alternative learning methods increasing the effort for lecturers. However, blended learning approaches enable the lecturers to separate these efforts and concentrate on the provisioning of alternative learning tasks before the semester, leaving sufficient time for lecturing during the semester. Regarding the teaching evaluation, the personalised flipped classroom course ANM was evaluated to be the fourth best course taught at the Faculty of Business, Economics and Social Sciences of the University of Hohenheim in the winter term 2017 (Department Information Systems 1 2017), showing very high student satisfaction. However, attendance of the course was perceived to be lower than in previous years, probably showing a divide between flip-endorsers, who constantly prepared, attended and therefore evaluated the lectures, and flip-resisters, who did not attend the course because of the extensive online materials provided or the high degree of interactivity required (McNally et al. 2017).

Finally, the proposed evaluation concept focuses on the achievement of the postulated requirements (i.e. COI; Arbaugh et al. 2008), learning outcomes (i.e. ISSM; DeLone and McLean 1992; Liaw and Huang 2013), adoption (i.e. TAM; Venkatesh and Bala 2008), and individual differences (i.e. MSLQ; Duncan and McKeachie 2005). It thereby incorporates models and instruments from the domains of the learning sciences as well as ISs research leading to a holistic concept for evaluation. From a practical, as well as research perspective, such an integration of theories and instruments is necessary. Teaching in higher education institutions becomes more and more permeated by electronic and blended learning methods, scientific evaluation and teaching evaluation for the purpose of quality assurance are left behind, if they do not incorporate the complete picture.

Therefore, this thesis makes a first step into combining theories and instruments from the learning sciences and ISs research as the two most important research disciplines in this environment.

6.2 Outlook

The present thesis analyses influence factors of personalised learning aiming to lay out design principles for personalised blended learning courses. Beginning with the analysis of learning styles, the thesis finds only weak support for a matching hypothesis between learning styles and specific teaching methods. Therefore, learning tasks – as clearly observable measures – are defined as the object of further investigations, instead of the psychometric properties of learning styles. Following the idea of a COI the PLF is developed, modelling personalised learning as a process of selection and usage of learning tasks and learning tools by the COI based on the theory of cognitive fit. Furthermore, the importance of institutional and contextual moderating variables is highlighted in the framework. The PLF represents the answer to the first research question stated in this thesis, presenting a comprehensive framework of influence factors regarding personalised learning. To evaluate the PLF further, a traditional university course is transformed to a personalised flipped classroom course using the PLF as a basis. Following an explanatory design theory, general requirements and general components are derived from the framework and implemented. This proof-of-concept course is successfully implemented and taught over a complete semester. Finally, an evaluation concept is presented, aiming to evaluate the PLF as a general framework as well as its instantiation in the personalised flipped classroom course highlighting self-regulated learning, learning outcomes, adoption of learning tools, and individual factors. Together the course design, implementation, and evaluation concept answer research question 2 showing how personalised learning can be supported in concrete learning interventions using specific learning methods and technologies.

6.2.1 Implications for Practitioners

Firstly, the thesis at hand is directed at teachers and learners involved in designing and implementing learning interventions. Secondly, the implications of this work might also be helpful to producers of VLEs opening new avenues for their development and marketing. Finally, it is relevant to educational institutions namely higher education institutions teaching degree-seeking students and companies engaging in the provision of professional trainings respectively human resource development providing in-house trainings. If such institutions are publicly funded the results of this thesis are also relevant to policy makers.

Teachers can use the presented requirements and components as blueprints for developing new courses in different domains providing personalised learning in a scalable manner. While personalisation always means extending existing course contents and didactics, e-learning is able to reduce the effort during teaching shifting it into the preparation phase. In the preparation phase, the flipped classroom increases online student retention due to its personalised approach and formative assessment. In the aspired setting of open communication and interactive discourse inside and outside the classroom student feedback is much more frequent as well as from higher quality.

From a learners' point of view, self-regulated personalised blended learning provides high availability and repeatability of course materials. Learners are free to choose where and when to prepare for the lectures. Furthermore, motivation has been found to be particularly low in online-only courses due to missing social context, delayed feedback, or unclear learning objectives (Renner et al. 2015). This leads to high drop-out rates for example in massive open online courses (Fox 2013). The flipped classroom process model including preparation and lecture phases provides a clear structure for learning objectives and feedback. Moreover, increased responsibility due to the self-regulated approach has also been found to benefit the learner's motivation (Zimmerman 2002). In the end, self-regulated personalised learning enables learning how to learn. Such metacognitive knowledge can be transferred to other courses or trainings.

Regarding the producers of VLEs, the requirements postulated in this thesis could influence future development of such systems. Its theoretical basis building on learning tasks and tools directly address features of VLEs regarding collaboration and communication and their interoperability with other (social media) tools forming a PLE. Furthermore, links between personalised learning and the more mature discipline of personalisation in e-commerce have been pointed out enabling the exaptation of e-commerce solutions in VLEs supporting personalised learning. For example, personalisation in e-commerce has been found to increase customer-loyalty and retention in online shops (Riemer 2002). Such approaches can be transferred to e-learning increasing retention for VLEs or other e-learning tools. Moreover, methods used to guide users in online shops, such as recommender systems, can be employed supporting personalised learning. While such recommendations are performed by the lecturers in the presented concept, they might be automated on the basis of learning data tracked in previous learning interventions in order to recommend specific learning tasks or learning tools based on individual preferences (Damiani et al. 2015).

For educational institutions and policy makers, the implementation of self-regulated personalisation is the next step towards competence-based life-long learning. Self-regulated personalisation puts more responsibility on the learners focusing on the collaborative and situated application of knowledge, while employing PLEs encourages them to build their own individually-tailored set of tools for learning extending the needs of single trainings or courses. The seamless integration of e-learning tools might require extensive infrastructure and support for the learners, however, provides an additional avenue to improve the learner's digital literacy alongside other learning outcomes. For their students personalised learning promises increased efficiency of learning tailored to their individual preferences using the PLF. For educational institutions themselves, an extended evaluation concept including models from the learning sciences as well as models from ISs research provides a holistic method to measure the success of their products.

All aforementioned groups of practitioners can benefit from an integration of self-regulated and automated approaches to personalised learning. Learning analytics, meaning the automated tracking of educational data (i.e. usage statistics, natural language, scores, etc.) to investigate learning behaviour and derive consequences, enables numerous applications to measure personalised learning regarding whether and how specific learning tasks and tools are used (Greller and Drachsler 2012). Educational institutions or policy makers could inform their strategy development regarding procurement of e-learning tools and curriculum development. Teachers could reflect on their courses and adapt them according to the tracked information and recommendations. Learners could receive personalised warnings if they fall behind or are in danger of dropping out of a course. Producers of VLEs could use the learning analytics data to improve their systems and evaluate new features. Particularly interesting is the idea of the quantified self (Swan 2012) asking the learners themselves to track their learning behaviour in the process of learning. The PLF could serve as the theoretical basis for a continuous tracking of learning tasks and learning tools using a mobile application or wearable (Rivera Pelayo 2015). Such an application is relevant for students but could also be employed for life-long learning or in professional trainings – irrespective of specific institutions. Based on tracked learning data such a system could provide statistics on the learning process, comparisons to other learners, and recommendations how to improve learning.

6.2.2   Implications for Researchers

Direct implications for future research lie in the systematic variation of the designed course concept according to different contents (i.e. within and across study programmes), learners (i.e. undergraduate, graduate, professional), institution (i.e. cooperative state university, university of applied sciences, university), and educational system respectively culture. By systematically comparing the experiences and results, general requirements could be verified and extended while general components could be clarified with specific characteristics.

Since the application of cognitive fit in personalised learning is an all new approach presented in this thesis, future research needs to disentangle the complex relationships between personalisation of tasks and tools. This includes an isolation of the impact of cognitive fit on the learning performance in general as well as an analysis of the two interdependent processes of cognitive fit regarding learning tasks and learning tools. Whilst this thesis follows a DBR methodology, controlled laboratory experiments are more suitable to isolate and investigate these relationships in greater detail, explaining their antecedents and characteristics. Previous literature on such interdependent effects, states the danger of interference (Shaft and Vessey 2006). Additionally, task-technology fit is integrated into the PLF, opening another dimension of fit, which probably leads to further interference. Furthermore, cognitive load theory has been applied to education and might be interesting to investigate as a complementary theory for personalised learning (van Merrienboer and Sweller 2010).

Another domain for future research is the number of learners under analysis. While cognitive fit and task-technology fit are only investigated for individuals in the literature, the PLF models personalised learning as an inherently collaborative endeavour represented as a COI. However, neither cognitive fit nor task-technology fit have been investigated in group decision-making. The learners need to find a compromise decision among each other regarding learning tasks and learning tools, which cannot satisfy all of them at once. Furthermore, interference between cognitive fit and task-technology fit are possible. It is, therefore, necessary to investigate how individual fit evolves to group fit regarding the selection and usage of specific learning tasks and learning tools (Gross et al. 2016; Ganzert et al. 2017). Besides this conceptual perspective, implementation and support of such group decision-making remains an area for future research in the realm of computer-supported collaborative work. How can collaborative learning be supported in VLEs in a personalised way?

Finally, self-regulated personalised learning is closely connected to learning motivation. While increased responsibility, group work, and structured preparation for the lecture foster intrinsic motivation, formative assessment benefits extrinsic motivation. Gamification (i.e. applying game-like elements to non-game concepts) represents an approach, which shares several characteristics with the flipped classroom. For example, gamification incorporates collaboration, situated tasks and application of knowledge in an immersive environment. Gamification has been found to increase intrinsic as well as extrinsic motivation, for example by introducing exploration (i.e. story-telling), competition (i.e. leader boards, badges), challenges (i.e. tasks, time-pressure), or collaboration (group tasks) (Blohm and Leimeister 2013). Introducing gamification elements, albeit following a well-structured concept, might therefore be a complementing approach, to improve self-regulated personalised learning even further.

Appendix A: Survey Items for Face-To-Face and E-Negotiation Skill Acquisition

Table 15   Survey Items for Face-To-Face and E-Negotiation Skill Acquisition

Construct	Item	
Negotiation Skill Acquisition	NEGOXP_1	I intuitively know how to negotiate.
	NEGOXP_2R (excluded)	When it comes to negotiations I do not know what to do.
	NEGOXP_3	I like to negotiate.
	NEGOXP_4R (excluded)	The underlying concepts of negotiations are difficult to understand.
	NEGOXP_5	I know how to use my negotiation knowledge for my advantage in negotiations.
	NEGOXP_6 (excluded)	I am familiar with negotiation concepts.
E-Negotiation Skill Acquisition	NSSXP_1	I intuitively know how to use the Negoisst system.
	NSSXP_2R	When it comes to negotiations with the Negoisst system I do not know what to do.
	NSSXP_3 (excluded)	I like to negotiate using the Negoisst system.
	NSSXP_4R	The underlying concepts of the Negoisst system are difficult to understand.
	NSSXP_5 (excluded)	I know how to use my knowledge of the Negoisst system for my advantage in electronic negotiations.
	NSSXP_6	I am familiar with the concepts of the Negoisst system.

© Springer Fachmedien Wiesbaden GmbH, part of Springer Nature 2019
P. Melzer, *A Conceptual Framework for Personalised Learning*,
https://doi.org/10.1007/978-3-658-23095-1

References

Abeysekera L, Dawson P (2014) Motivation and Cognitive Load in the Flipped Classroom: Definition, Rationale and a Call for Research. Higher Education Research & Development, 34(1):1–14

Acton T, Scott M, Hill S (2005) E-Education – Keys to Success for Organisations. Proceedings of 18th Bled eConference: eIntegration in Action, 8-6-2005

Adair WL, Brett J (2005) The Negotiation Dance: Time, Culture, and Behavioral Sequences in Negotiation, Organization Science 16(1):33–51

Adams Becker S, Cummins M, Davis A, Freeman A, Hall Giesinger C, Ananthanarayanan V (2017) NMC Horizon Report: 2017 Higher Education Edition. Available at: http://cdn.nmc.org/media/2017-nmc-horizon-report-he-EN.pdf Accessed 5-26-2017

Allinson CW, Hayes J (1988) The Learning Style Questionnaire: An Alternative to Kolb's Inventory? Journal of Management Studies 25(3):269–281

Alonso F, Manrique D, Viñes JM (2009) A Moderate Constructivist E-Learning Instructional Model Evaluated on Computer Specialists, Computers & Education 53(1):57–65

Anderson JR, Boyle CF, Reiser BJ (1985). Intelligent Tutoring Systems. Science, 228(4698):456–462

Anderson LW, Krathwohl DR (2001) A Taxonomy for Learning, Teaching, and Assessing: A Revision of Bloom's Taxonomy of Educational Objectives, Longman, New York, USA

Anderson T, Shattuck J (2012) Design-Based Research: A Decade of Progress in Education Research? Educational Researcher 41(1):16–25

Andersson A, Hedstrom K, Gronlund A (2009) Learning from eLearning: Emerging Constructive Learning Practices, in Proceedings of the International Conference on Information Systems (ICIS) 2009, Phoenix, USA, n.d., paper 51

Andriessen J. (2006) Arguing to Learn. In: Sawyer RK (ed.) The Cambridge Handbook of the Learning Sciences, Cambridge University Press, Cambridge, UK, pp 443–459

Arbaugh JB, Cleveland-Innes M, Diaz SR, Garrison DR, Ice P, Richardson JC, Swan KP (2008) Developing a Community of Inquiry Instrument: Testing a Measure of the Community of Inquiry Framework Using a Multi-Institutional Sample. The Internet and Higher Education, 11(3-4):133–136

© Springer Fachmedien Wiesbaden GmbH, part of Springer Nature 2019
P. Melzer, *A Conceptual Framework for Personalised Learning*,
https://doi.org/10.1007/978-3-658-23095-1

Attwell G (2007) Personal Learning Environments – The Future of eLearning? eLearning Papers 2(1)

Azevedo R, Moos DC, Greene JA, Winters FI, Cromley JG (2008) Why is externally-facilitated regulated learning more effective than self-regulated learning with hypermedia? Educational Technology Research and Development 56(1):45–72

Bandura A (1977) Social Learning Theory. Prentice Hall, Englewood Cliffs, USA

Bandura A (1989) Human Agency in Social Cognitive Theory. American Psychologist, 44(9):1175–1184

Barab S (2006) Design-Based Research. In: Sawyer, K.R. (ed.). The Cambridge Handbook of the Learning Sciences. Cambridge University Press, Cambridge, USA, pp. 153–169

Barab S, Squire K (2004) Design-Based Research: Putting a Stake in the Ground. Journal of the Learning Sciences, 13(1):1–14

Baskerville R, Myers MD (2004). Special Issue on Action Research in Information Systems: Making IS Research Relevant to Practice: Foreword. Management Information Systems Quarterly, 28(3):329–335

Baskerville RL, Pries-Heje J (2010) Explanatory Design Theory. Business & Information Systems Engineering, 2(5):271–282

Ben-Yoav O, Banai M (1992) Measuring Conflict Management Styles: A Comparison between the MODE and ROC-II Instruments Using Self and Peer Ratings. International Journal of Conflict Management 3(3):237–247

Berglar P (1970). Wilhelm von Humboldt in Selbstzeugnissen und Bilddokumenten. Rowohlts Monographien [161]. Rowohlt, Reinbek, Germany

Bichler M, Kersten G, Strecker S (2003) Towards a Structured Design of Electronic Negotiations, Group Decision and Negotiation 12(4):311–335

Bill and Melinda Gates Foundation (2014) Early Progress Interim Research on Personalized Learning: RAND Corporation. Available at: http://k12education.gatesfoundation.org/wp-content/uploads/2015/06/Early-Progress-on-Personalized-Learning-Full-Report.pdf Accessed 5-26-2017

Bing W, Ping TA (2008) A Comparative Analysis of Learners Interaction in the Online Learning Management Systems: Does National Culture Matter? Asian Association of Open Universities Journal, 3(1):1–16

Bishop JL, Verleger MA (2013) The Flipped Classroom: A Survey of the Research. Proceedings of the 120th ASEE Annual Conference & Exposition, Atlanta, USA, 6-26-2013

Blake RR, Mouton JS (1964) The Managerial Grid. Gulf, Houston, USA

Blohm I, Leimeister JM (2013) Gamification. Wirtschaftsinformatik, 55(4):275–278

Bloom BS, Krathwohl DR, Masia BB (1984) Taxonomy of Educational Objectives: The Classification of Educational Goals, Vol. 1. Longman, New York, USA

Bönsch M (2016) Heterogenität verlangt Differenzierung. Zeitschrift für Bildungsverwaltung, 32(1):11–21

Boondao R, Hurst AJ, Sheard JI (2008) Understanding Cultural Influences: Principles for Personalized E-learning Systems. Proceedings of World Academy of Science: Engineering & Technology, Vol. 48, p. 1326, 12-2008

Bostrom RP, Olfman L, Sein MK (1990) The Importance of Learning Style in End-User Training. MIS Quarterly 14(1):101–119

Bower M, Hedberg JG, Kuswara A (2010) A Framework for Web 2.0 Learning Design, Educational Media International 47(3)177–198.

Brown AL (1992) Design Experiments: Theoretical and Methodological Challenges in Creating Complex Interventions in Classroom Settings. Journal of the Learning Sciences 2(2):141–178

Brown JS, Adler RP (2008) Minds on Fire: Open Education, the Long Tail, and Learning 2.0. EDUCAUSE Review, 43(1):16–32

Buchem I, Attwell G, Torres R (2011) Understanding Personal Learning Environments: Literature Review and Synthesis Through the Activity Theory Lens. In: Proceedings of the PLE Conference, Southampton, UK, pp. 1–33

Butt A (2014) Student Views on the Use of a Flipped Classroom Approach: Evidence from Australia. Business Education & Accreditation 6(1):33–44

Cassidy S (2004) Learning Styles an Overview of Theories, Models, and Measures. Educational Psychology, 24(4):419–444

Chan T, Rosemann M, Tan SY (2014) Identifying Satisfaction Factors in Tertiary Education: The Case of an Information Systems Program. In: Myers, M Straub, D (eds.) Proceedings of the International Conference on Information Systems (ICIS) 2014, Auckland, New Zealand. 12-17-2014

Chen BH, Chiou HH (2014) Learning Style, Sense of Community and Learning Effectiveness in Hybrid Learning Environment. Interactive Learning Environment, 22(4):485–496

Chiu CM, Chiu CS, Chang HC (2007) Examining the Integrated Influence of Fairness and Quality on Students' Satisfaction and Web-based Learning Continuance Intention. Information Systems Journal 17(3):271–287

Churches A (2009) Bloom's Digital Taxonomy. Available at: http://edorigami.wikispaces.com/file/view/bloom%27s%20Digital%20taxonomy%20v3.01.pdf/65720266/bloom%27s%20Digital%20taxonomy%20v3.01.pdf Accessed 4-28-2015

CLEX (2009) Higher Education in a Web 2.0 World. http://www.webarchive.org.uk/wayback/archive/20140614042502/http://www.jisc.ac.uk/publications/generalpublications/2009/heweb2.aspx Accessed 4-27-2015

Coffield F, Moseley D, Hall E, Ecclestone K (2004) Learning Styles and Pedagogy in Post-16 Learning: A Systematic and Critical Review, Learning and Skills Research Centre, London, UK

Collins A (1992) Toward a Design Science of Education. In: Scanlon E O'Shea T (eds.) New Directions in Educational Technology. 96:15–22. NATO ASI Series: Springer, Berlin, Germany

Collins A, Joseph D, Bielaczyc K (2004) Design Research: Theoretical and Methodological Issues, Journal of the Learning Sciences 13(1)15–42

Confrey J (2006) The Evolution of Design Studies as Methodology. In: Sawyer KR (ed.). The Cambridge Handbook of the Learning Sciences. Cambridge University Press, Cambridge, USA, pp. 135–151

Cronbach LJ (1951) Coefficient Alpha and the Internal Structure of Tests. Psychometrika 16(3):297–334

Damiani E, Ceravolo P, Frati F, Bellandi V, Maier R, Seeber I, Waldhart G (2015) Applying Recommender Systems in Collaboration Environments. Computers in Human Behavior 51:1124–1133

Davis SA, Bostrom RP (1993) Training End Users: An Experimental Investigation of the Roles of the Computer Interface and Training Methods. MIS Quarterly 17(1):61–85

Day JA, Foley JD (2006) Evaluating a Web Lecture Intervention in a Human-Computer Interaction Course. IEEE Transactions on Education 49(4):420–431

De Dreu CK, Boles TL (1998) Share and Share Alike or Winner Take All? The Influence of Social Value Orientation upon Choice and Recall of Negotiation Heuristics. Organizational Behavior and Human Decision Processes 76(3):253–276

De Moura JA, Seixas Costa APC (2014) Incorporating Personal Style into a Negotiation Support System. In: Zaraté P, Camilleri G, Kamissoko D, Amblard F (eds.) Proceedings of Group Decision and Negotiation Conference 2014, Toulouse, France, pp. 95–99

Dekker S, Lee NC, Howard-Jones P, Jolles J (2012) Neuromyths in Education: Prevalence and Predictors of Misconceptions among Teachers. Frontiers in Psychology 3:429

Delaney MM, Foroughi A, Perkins WC (1997) An Empirical Study of the Efficacy of a Computerized Negotiation Support System (NSS). Decision Support Systems 20(3):185–197

DeLone WH, McLean ER (1992) Information Systems Success: The Quest for the Dependent Variable. Information Systems Research 3(1):60–95

DeLone WH, McLean ER (2003) The DeLone and McLean Model of Information Systems Success: A Ten-Year Update. Journal of Management Information Systems 19(4):9–30

Department Information Systems 1 2017 Auszeichnung in der Lehre V. Available at: https://wi1.uni-hohenheim.de/103553?tx_ttnews%5Btt_news%5D=36736&cHash=62a683b8fb4cbbf074b5ffc8a975d649 Accessed 8-23-2017

Dewey J (1893) Self-Realization as the Moral Ideal, The Philosophical Review 2:652–664. Available at https://ia801701.us.archive.org/26/items/jstor-2176020/2176020.pdf Accessed 5-28-2018

Dewey J (1997) How We Think, Dover Publications, Mineola, USA

Dewey J (2013) Logic: The Theory of Inquiry. Read Books Ltd

Downes S (2005) E-Learning 2.0, eLearn 2005(10)

Duff A, Duffy T (2002) Psychometric Properties of Honey & Mumford's Learning Styles Questionnaire (LSQ). Personality and Individual Differences 33(1):147–163

Duncan TG, McKeachie WJ (2005) The Making of the Motivated Strategies for Learning Survey. Educational Psychologist 40(2):117–128

EDUCAUSE Learning Initiative (2012) 7 Things You Should Know About Flipped Classrooms. Available at: https://net.educause.edu/ir/library/pdf/eli7081.pdf Accessed 11-4-2016

Eliashberg J, Gauvin S, Lilien GL, Rangaswamy A (1992) An Experimental Study of Alternative Preparation Aids for International Negotiations, Group Decision and Negotiation 1(3):243–267

Emerson R (2013) Powering Smart Content for Publishing Giants, Knewton Lands $51M to Take Personalized Learning Global. Available at: http://techcrunch.com/2013/12/19/powering-smart-content-for-publishing-giants-knewton-lands-51m-to-take-its-personalization-engine-global/ Accessed 2-9-2015

Erpenbeck J, Hasebrook J (2011) Sind Kompetenzen Persönlichkeitseigenschaften? In: Faix WG (ed.). Kompetenz, Persönlichkeit, Bildung (1. Aufl.). Steinbeis-Edition, Stuttgart, Germany, pp. 227–262

Erpenbeck J, Sauter W (2013) So werden wir lernen! Kompetenzentwicklung in einer Welt fühlender Computer, kluger Wolken und sinnsuchender Netze. Springer Gabler, Berlin, Germany

European Commission (2014) Horizon 2020 – Topic: Technologies for Better Human Learning and Teaching. http://ec.europa.eu/research/participants/portal/desktop/en/opportunities/h2020/topics/ict-20-2015.html

Eymann T, Kundisch D, Recker J, Bernstein A, Gebauer J, Günther O, Ketter W, zur Mühlen M, Riemer K (2014) Should I Stay or Should I Go. Wirtschaftsinformatik, 56(2):131–144

Falmagne JC, Cosyn E, Doignon JP, Thiéry N (2006) The Assessment of Knowledge, in Theory and in Practice. In: Hutchison D, Kanade T, Kittler J, Kleinberg JM, Mattern F, Mitchell JC, Naor M, Nierstrasz O, Pandu Rangan C, Steffen B, Sudan M, Terzopoulos D, Tygar D, Vardi MY, Weikum G, Missaoui R, Schmidt J (eds.) Formal Concept Analysis. Springer, Berlin, Germany, pp. 61–79

Feldstein M, Hill P (2016) Personalized Learning: What It Really Is and Why It Really Matters. EDUCAUSE Review, 51(2)

Field AP (2013) Discovering Statistics Using IBM SPSS Statistics: And Sex and Drugs and Rock 'n' Roll, 4th ed. Sage, Los Angeles, USA

Findlay-Thompson S, Mombourquette P (2014) Evaluation of a Flipped Classroom in an Undergraduate Business Course. Business Education & Accreditation 6(1):63–71

Fox A (2013) From MOOCs to SPOCs. Communications of the ACM, 56(12):38–40

Fredricks JA, McColskey W (2012) The Measurement of Student Engagement. A Comparative Analysis of Various Methods and Student Self-

Report Instruments. Christenson SL Reschly AL Wylie C (eds.), Handbook of Research on Student Engagement. Springer, Boston, USA, pp. 763–782

Galbraith MW (2004) Adult Learning Methods: A Guide for Effective Instruction. 3rd Edition Krieger Pub. Co., Malabar, USA

Ganzert M, Huber S, Kaya M, Melzer P, Schoop M, Sepin S (2017) Adoption, Usage, and Pedagogy of E-Learning Tools in University Teaching. Proceedings of UK Academy for Information Systems Conference, 4-5-2017 Oxford, UK, paper 19

Garrison DR (2011) E-learning in the 21st Century. A Framework for Research and Practice. 2nd ed. Routledge, New York, USA

Garrison DR, Arbaugh JB (2007) Researching the Community of Inquiry Framework: Review, Issues, and Future Directions. The Internet and Higher Education 10(3):157–72

Garrison DR, ND Vaughan (2011) Blended Learning in Higher Education: Framework, Principles, and Guidelines, Jossey-Bass, San Francisco, USA

Gayer C, Müller B (2015) Ergebnisse der Online-Umfrage zur Umstellung auf ILIAS. http://blog.lehrentwicklung.uni-freiburg.de/2015/02/ergebnisse-der-online-umfrage-zur-umstellung-auf-ilias/ Accessed 11-4-2016

Gettinger J, Dannenmann A, Druckman D, Filzmoser M, Mitterhofer R, Reiser A, Schoop M, Vetschera R, Wijst P, Köszegi S (2012) Impact of and Interaction between Behavioral and Economic Decision Support in Electronic Negotiations. In: Hernández JE (ed.) Decision support systems – Collaborative models and approaches in real environments, Vol. 121. Springer, Berlin, Germany, pp. 151–165

Goodhue DL, Thompson RL (1995) Task-Technology Fit and Individual Performance, MIS Quarterly 19(2):213-236

Google Scholar (2017) Available at: www.scholar.google.de Accessed 3-13-2017

Graf S, List B (2005) An Evaluation of Open Source E-Learning Platforms Stressing Adaptation Issues. In: Fifth IEEE International Conference on Advanced Learning Technologies (ICALT'05), Kaohsiung, Taiwan, pp. 163–165, 07-08-2005

Green H, Facer K, Rudd T, Dillon P, Humphreys P (2005) Futurelab: Personalisation and Digital Technologies: Research Report, <hal-00190337>

Gregor S, Hevner AR (2013) Positioning and Presenting Design Science Research for Maximum Impact, Management Information Systems Quarterly 37(2):337–355

Greller W, Drachsler H (2012) Translating Learning into Numbers: A Generic Framework for Learning Analytics. Educational Technology & Society, 15(3):42–57

Gross P, Schmid A, Gettinger J, Melzer P, Schoop M (2016) How Do University Students Select and Use their Learning Tools? A Mixed-Method Study on Personalised Learning. In: Brooks L Wainwright D Wastell D (eds.), UK Academy of Information Systems Conference Proceedings 2016 (UKAIS 2016). UKAIS. Oxford, UK, 4-13-2016, paper 21

Gunasekaran A, McNeil RD, Shaul D (2002) E-Learning: Research and Applications. Industrial and Commercial Training, 34(2):44–53

Gupta S, Anson R (2014) Do I Matter? Journal of Organizational and End User Computing 26(2):60–79

Gupta S, Bostrom RP (2006) End-User Training Methods. In: Shayo C, Kaiser K, Ryan T (eds.) The 2006 ACM SIGMIS CPR Conference, Pomona, USA, pp. 172-182, 04-15-2006

Gupta S, Bostrom RP Huber M (2010) End-User Training Methods. ACM SIGMIS Database, 41(4):9-39

Habermas J (1984) The Theory of Communicative Action. Beacon Press, Boston, USA

Haggis T. (2003) Constructing Images of Ourselves? A Critical Investigation into 'Approaches to Learning' Research in Higher Education, British Educational Research Journal 29(1):89–104

Hair JF, Black WC, Babin BJ, Anderson RE (2010) Multivariate Data Analysis, 7th ed. Prentice Hall, Upper Saddle River, USA

Hair JF, Hult TG, Ringle C, Sarstedt M (2014) A Primer on Partial Least Squares Structural Equations Modelling (PLS-SEM). Sage, Los Angeles, USA

Harel I, Papert S (1993) Constructionism: Research Reports and Essays, 1985-1990. 2nd ed. ABLEX Publishing Corporation, Norwood, USA

Heggestuen J (2013) One in Every 5 People in the World Own a Smartphone, one in Every 17 Own a Tablet. Available at: http://www.businessinsider.com/smartphone-and-tablet-penetration-2013-10 Accessed 4-23-2014

Hevner AR, March ST Park J, Ram S (2004) Design Science in Information Systems Research, MIS Quarterly 28(1):75–106

Hill P (2015) State of the US Higher Education LMS Market: 2015 Edition. Available at: http://mfeldstein.com/state-of-the-us-higher-education-LMS-market-2015-edition/ Accessed 4-15-2017

Hill T, Chidambaram L, Summers JD (2016) Playing 'Catch Up' with Blended Learning: Performance Impacts of Augmenting Classroom Instruction with Online Learning. Behaviour & Information Technology, pp. 1–9

Hirshon A (2005) A Diamond in the Rough: Divining the Future of E-Content, EDUCAUSE Review 40(1):34–44

Hofstede GH (1984) Culture's Consequences: International Differences in Work-Related Values, Abridged ed. Sage, Los Angeles, USA

Honey P, Mumford A (1992) The Manual of Learning Styles, 3rd ed. Peter Honey Learning, Maidenhead, UK

Honey P, Mumford A (1992) Using Your Learning Styles: Psychology Press

Honey P, Mumford A (2000) The Learning Styles Helper's Guide. Peter Honey Learning, Maidenhead, UK

Huber GP (1983) Cognitive Style as a Basis for MIS and DSS Designs: Much Ado About Nothing? Management Science 29(5):567–579

Igbaria M, Guimaraes T, Davis GB (1995) Testing the Determinants of Microcomputer Usage via a Structural Equation Model. Journal of Management Information Systems 11(4):87–114

ILIAS e.V. (2016) ILIAS Homepage. Available at: http://www.ilias.de Accessed 11-7-2016

Johnson L, Adams Becker S, Cummins M, Estrada V, Freeman A, Hall C (2016) NMC Horizon Report: 2016: Higher Education Edition. Austin, USA: New Media Consortium, Available at: http://cdn.nmc.org/media/2016-nmc-horizon-report-he-EN.pdf Accessed 2-16-2016

Johnson L, Adams Becker S, Estrada V, Freeman A (2015) The NMC Horizon Report: 2015 Higher Education Edition. Austin, USA: New Media Consortium Available at: http://cdn.nmc.org/media/2015-nmc-horizon-report-HE-EN.pdf Accessed 2-18-2015

Johnson RB, Onwuegbuzie AJ, (2004) Mixed Methods Research: A Research Paradigm Whose Time Has Come. Educational Researcher, 33(7):14–26

Jonassen DH (1990) Thinking Technology: Toward a Constructivist View of Instructional Design, Educational Technology 30(9):32–34

Jung CG (1923) Psychological Types. 1. ed.: Kegan Paul, Trench, Trubner & Co., Ltd

Kafai YB (2006) Constructionism. In: Sawyer KR (ed.) The Cambridge Handbook of the Learning Sciences, pp. 35–46, Cambridge University Press, Cambridge, UK

Kafai YB (2006) Constructionism. In: Sawyer KR (ed.), The Cambridge Handbook of the Learning Sciences, Cambridge University Press, Cambridge, UK, pp. 35–46

Katz IR, Macklin AS (2007) Information and Communication Technology (ICT) Literacy: Integration and Assessment in Higher Education. http://www.iiisci.org/Journal/CV$/sci/pdfs/P890541.pdf Accessed 5-1-2015

Kaufman (1998) Using Simulation as a Tool to Teach About International Negotiation, International Negotiation 3(1):59–75

Keeney RL, Raiffa H (1976) Decisions with Multiple Objectives: Preferences and Value Trade-Offs. Wiley Series in Probability and Mathematical Statistics. Wiley, New York, USA

Kilmann RH, Thomas KW (1992) Conflict MODE Instrument, 35th ed. Mountain View, USA

Kiy A, Lucke U (2016) Technical Approaches for Personal Learning Environments: Identifying Archetypes from a Literature Review. In: Spector MJ Tsai CC Sampson DG Kinshuk Ronghuai H Chen NS Resta P (eds.), Proceedings of the 16th IEEE International Conference on Advanced Learning Technologies (ICALT), Krakow, Poland, 06-03-2016

Koedinger KR, Corbett AT (2006) Cognitive Tutors: Technology Bringing Learning Sciences to the Classroom. In: Sawyer, K.R. (ed.). The Cambridge Handbook of the Learning Sciences. Cambridge University Press, Cambridge, UK, pp. 61–77

Kolb AY, Kolb DA (2005) The Kolb Learning Style Inventory—Version 3.1 2005 Technical Specifications: Hay Group: Experience Based Learning Systems, Inc. Available at: http://learningfromexperience.com/media/2010/08/Tech_spec_LSI.pdf Accessed 5-26-2017

Kolb DA (1984) Experiential Learning: Experience as a Source of Learning and Development. Prentice-Hall, Englewood Cliffs, USA

Kolb DA (2000) Facilitator's Guide to Learning. Hay Group, n.p.

Köszegi S, Kersten G (2003) On-line/Off-line: Joint Negotiation Teaching in Montreal and Vienna. Group Decision and Negotiation 12(4):337–345

Krathwohl DR (2002) A Revision of Bloom's Taxonomy: An Overview. Theory into Practice, 41(4):212–218

Krieg J, Maier L, Schreiber M (2017) How to Learn to Negotiate: An Interactive University Teaching Concept in Negotiation Management from a Students' Perspective. In: Schoop M Kilgour DM (eds.). Proceedings of 17th Conference on Group Decision and Negotiation. University of Hohenheim, Stuttgart, Germany, pp. 451–459

Kumar V, Graf SK (2011) Causal Competencies and Learning Styles: A Framework for Adaptive Instruction. Journal of E-Learning and Knowledge Society, 7(3)

Kunkel A, Bräutigam, P, Hatzelmann, E. (2006) Verhandeln nach Drehbuch: Aus Hollywood-Filmen für eigene Verhandlungen lernen, Redline Wirtschaft, Heidelberg, Germany

Lage MJ, Platt GJ, Treglia M (2000) Inverting the Classroom: A Gateway to Creating an Inclusive Learning Environment. The Journal of Economic Education 31(1):30–43

Lambert JL, Fisher JL (2013) Community of Inquiry Framework: Establishing Community in an Online Course. Journal of Interactive Online Learning, 12(1):1–16

Lave J, Wenger E (1991) Situated Learning: Legitimate Peripheral Participation, Cambridge University Press, Cambridge, UK

Lee YC (2006) An Empirical Investigation into Factors Influencing the Adoption of an E-Learning System. Online Information Review 30(5):517–541

Lehmann K, Oeste S, Janson A, Söllner M, Leimeister JM (2015) Flipping the Classroom – IT-unterstützte Lerneraktivierung zur Verbesserung des Lernerfolges einer universitären Massenlehrveranstaltung. HMD Praxis der Wirtschaftsinformatik, 52(1):81–95

Lehmann K, Söllner, M (2014) Theory-Driven Design of a Mobile-Learning Application to Support Different Interaction Types in Large-Scale Lectures. In: Avital M, Leimeister JM, and Schultze U (eds.) Proceedings of the European Conference (ECIS) 2014: 22th European Conference on Information Systems; Tel Aviv, Israel, 6-11-2014, AIS Electronic Library

Leidenfrost B, Strassnig B, Schabmann A, Carbon CC (2009) Verbesserung der Studiensituation für StudienanfängerInnen durch Cascaded Blended Mentoring. Psychologische Rundschau, 60(2):99–106

Levine TR, Hullett CR (2002) Eta Squared, Partial Eta Squared, and Misreporting of Effect Size in Communication Research. Human Communication Research 28(4):612–625

Lewicki R (1997) Teaching Negotiation and Dispute Resolution in Colleges of Business: The State of the Practice, Negotiation Journal 13(3):253–269

Liaw SS, Huang HM (2013) Perceived Satisfaction, Perceived Usefulness and Interactive Learning Environments as Predictors to Self-Regulation in E-Learning Environments. Computers & Education 60(1):14–24

Loewenstein J, Thompson LL (2006) Learning to Negotiate: Novice and Experienced Negotiators. In: Thompson, LL (ed.), Negotiation Theory and Research, Psychology Press, New York, USA, pp. 77–97

Lu HP, Chiou MJ (2010) The Impact of Individual Factors on E-Learning System Satisfaction: A Contingency Approach. British Journal of Educational Technology 41(2):307–323

Ma Z, Liang D, Erkus A, Tabak A (2012) The Impact of Group-Oriented Values on Choice of Conflict Management Styles and Outcomes: An Empirical Study in Turkey. The International Journal of Human Resource Management 23(18):3776–3793

Marsick VJ, Watkins KE (2001) Informal and Incidental Learning. New Directions for Adult and Continuing Education, 2001 (89):25

Mazur E (1997) Peer Instruction: A User's Manual, Prentice Hall, Upper Saddle River, USA

McGill TJ, Hobbs VJ (2008) How Students and Instructors Using a Virtual Learning Environment Perceive the Fit between Technology and Task. Journal of Computer Assisted Learning, 24(3):191–202

McGill TJ, Klobas JE (2009) A Task–Technology Fit View of Learning Management System Impact. Computers & Education, 52(2):496–508

McLafferty I (2004) Focus Group Interviews as a Data Collecting Strategy. Journal of Advanced Nursing 48(2):187–194

McLaughlin JE, Roth MT, Glatt DM, Gharkholonarehe N, Davidson CA, Griffin LM, Esserman DA, Mumper RJ (2014) The Flipped Classroom: A Course Redesign to Foster Learning and Engagement in a Health Professions School. Academic Medicine: Journal of the Association of American Medical Colleges, 89(2):236–243

McLoughlin C, Lee MJ (2010) Personalised and Self-Regulated Learning in the Web 2.0 Era: International Exemplars of Innovative Pedagogy

Using Social Software, Australasian Journal of Educational Technology 26(1):28–43

McNally B, Chipperfield J, Dorsett P, Del Fabbro L, Frommolt V, Goetz S, Lewohl J, Molineux M, Pearson A, Reddan G, Roiko A, Rung A (2017) Flipped Classroom Experiences: Student Preferences and Flip Strategy in a Higher Education Context. Higher Education 73(2):281–98

Mead GH (1913) The Social Self. The Journal of Philosophy, Psychology and Scientific Methods, 10(14):374

Meiers R (2012) Die Einführung von Learning Management Systemen an deutschen Hochschulen: Fördernde und hemmende Faktoren. Dissertation, Philosophischen Fakultät II, Universität des Saarlandes, Saarbrücken, Germany

Melzer P, Schoop M (2014a) Individual End-User Training for Information Systems using Learning Styles. In Brooks L, Wainwright D, and Wastell D (eds.) UK Academy of Information Systems Conference Proceedings 2014 (UKAIS 2014), Oxford, UK. 4-9-2014

Melzer P, Schoop M (2014b) Towards Individual Negotiation Training for Negotiation Support Systems. In: Zaraté P, Camilleri G, Kamissoko D, Amblard F (eds.) Proceedings of Group Decision and Negotiation Conference 2014, Toulouse, France, 6-13-2014, pp. 40–45

Melzer P, Schoop M (2014c) Utilising Learning Methods in Electronic Negotiation Training. In: Kundisch D, Suhl L, Beckmann L (eds.) Proceedings of Multikonferenz Wirtschaftsinformatik, Paderborn, Germany 2-28-2014, pp. 776–788

Melzer P, Schoop M (2015) A Conceptual Framework for Task and Tool Personalisation in IS Education. In Leidner D, Ross J (eds.) Proceedings of the Thirty Sixth International Conference on Information Systems (ICIS 2015). IS Curriculum and Education, paper 6, Fort Worth, USA

Melzer P, Schoop M (2016) The Effects of Personalised Negotiation Training on Learning and Performance in Electronic Negotiations. Group Decision and Negotiation 25(6):1189–1210

Melzer P, Schoop M (2017a) Personalising the IS Classroom – Insights on Course Design and Implementation. Proceedings of the 25th European Conference on Information Systems (ECIS 2017), 6-10-2017 Guimaraes, Portugal, pp. 1391–1405

Melzer P, Schoop M (2017b) Towards a Holistic Evaluation Concept for Personalised Learning in Flipped Classrooms. In: Griffiths JM, McLean

R, Kutar M (eds.). Ubiquitous Information Systems: Surviving & Thriving in a Connected Society 2017. UKAIS, paper 21, Oxford, UK, 04-05-2017

Messick DM, McClintock CG (1968) Motivational Bases of Choice in Experimental Games. Journal of Experimental Social Psychology 4(1):1–25

Miller A (2012) 5 Best Practices for the Flipped Classroom. Available at: https://www.edutopia.org/blog/flipped-classroom-best-practices-andrew-miller Accessed 11-4-2016

Milman NB (2012) The Flipped Classroom Strategy What Is it and How Can it Best be Used? Distance Learning 9(3):85-75

Moore S (2016) Gartner Highlights Top 10 Strategic Technologies for Higher Education in 2016. Available at: http://www.gartner.com/newsroom/id/3225717 Accessed 2-21-2017

Moravec M, Williams A, Aguilar-Roca N, O'Dowd DK (2010) Learn Before Lecture: A Strategy That Improves Learning Outcomes in a Large Introductory Biology Class. CBE Life Sciences Education 9(4):473–481

Myers IB, McCaulley MH, Most R (1985) Manual, a Guide to the Development and Use of the Myers-Briggs Type Indicator. Consulting Psychologists Press, Palo Alto, USA

Narciss S, Proske A, Koerndle H (2007) Promoting Self-Regulated Learning in Web-Based Learning Environments, Computers in Human Behavior 23(3):1126–1144

Nunnally JC, Bernstein IH (1994) Psychometric Theory, 3rd ed., McGraw-Hill Series in Psychology. McGraw-Hill, New York, USA

Oeste S, Lehmann K, Janson A, Leimeister JM (2014) Flipping the IS Classroom – Theory-Driven Design for Large-Scale Lectures. In: Myers M Straub DW (eds.), Proceedings of the International Conference on Information Systems (ICIS) 2014. International Conference on Information Systems (ICIS). Auckland, New Zealand, 12-17-2014. AIS

Olekalns M, Smith PL (1999) Social Value Orientations and Strategy Choices in Competitive Negotiations. Personality and Social Psychology Bulletin 25(6):657–668

Pane JF, Steiner ED, Baird MD, Hamilton LS (2015) Continued Progress Promising Evidence on Personalized Learning: RAND Corporation, Available at: http://k12education.gatesfoundation.org/wp-content/uploads/2015/11/Gates-ContinuedProgress-Nov13.pdf Accessed 5-26-2017

Papert S (1993) Mindstorms: Children, Computers, and Powerful Ideas. 2nd ed. Basicbooks, New York, USA

Pappas C (2015) The Top LMS Statistics and Facts for 2015 You Need to Know. Available at: https://elearningindustry.com/top-lms-statistics-and-facts-for-2015 Accessed 4-15-2017

Parker J, Herrington J (2015) Setting the Climate in an Authentic Online Community of Learning. In: Bauley M (ed.), Proceedings of Australian Association for Research in Education (AARE) Conference 2015, Fremantle, Australia, 12-03-2015

Pashler H, McDaniel M, Rohrer D, Bjork R (2009) Learning Styles: Concepts and Evidence. Psychological Science in the Public Interest, 9(3):105–119

Persike M, Friedrich JD (2016) Lernen mit digitalen Medien aus Studierendenperspektive: Sonderauswertung aus dem CHE Hochschulranking für die deutschen Hochschulen Arbeitspapier Nr. 17), Available at: https://hochschulforumdigitalisierung.de/sites/default/files/dateien/HFD_AP_Nr_17_Lernen_mit_digitalen_Medien_aus_Studierendenperspektive.pdf Accessed 5-26-2017

Pesendorfer E, Köszegi ST (2006) Hot Versus Cool Behavioural Styles in Electronic Negotiations: The Impact of Communication Mode. Group Decision and Negotiation 15(2):141–155

Pierce R, Fox J (2012) Vodcasts and Active-Learning Exercises in a "Flipped Classroom" Model of a Renal Pharmacotherapy Module. American Journal of Pharmaceutical Education, 76(10):196

Pintrich PR, Marx RW, Boyle RA (1993) Beyond Cold Conceptual Change: The Role of Motivational Beliefs and Classroom Contextual Factors in the Process of Conceptual Change, Review of Educational Research 63(2):167–199

Pituch K, A Lee YK (2006) The Influence of System Characteristics on E-Learning Use. Computers & Education 47(2):222–244

Prensky M (2001) Digital Natives, Digital Immigrants Part 1. On the Horizon 9 (5): 1–6

Puentedura RR (2003) A Matrix Model for Designing and Assessing Network-Enhanced Courses. Available at: http://www.hippasus.com/resources/matrixmodel/ Accessed 12-3-2016

Raiffa H, Richardson J, Metcalfe D (2002) Negotiation Analysis: The Science and Art of Collaborative Decision Making. Belknap Press of Harvard University Press, Cambridge, USA

Renner D, Laumer S, Weitzel T (2015) Blended Learning Success: Cultural and Learning Style Impacts. Wirtschaftsinformatik Proceedings 2015.

Riemer K (2002) Personalisierung am Beispiel des Internet-Handels. In: Ahlert D Becker J Knacksted R Wunderlich M (eds.). Customer Relationship Management im Handel: Strategien – Konzepte – Erfahrungen. Springer, Berlin, Germany, pp. 103–128

Rivera Pelayo V (2015) Design and Application of Quantified Self Approaches for Reflective Learning in the Workplace, Dissertation, Karlsruher Institut für Technologie, Karlsruhe, Germany

Robey D, Taggart W (1981) Measuring Managers' Minds: The Assessment of Style in Human Information Processing. The Academy of Management Review 6(3):375–383

Robey D, Taggart W (1983) Issues in Cognitive Style Measurement: A Response to Schweiger. The Academy of Management Review 8(1):152–155

Ruble TL, Stout DE (1993) Learning Styles and End-User Training: An Unwarranted Leap of Faith. MIS Quarterly 17(1):115–118

Schaper E, Tipold A (2015) Erfolgreiche E-Learning-Szenarien in der universitären, veterinärmedizinischen Ausbildung. Hamburger eLearning-Magazin (14):26–27

Schoop M (2005) A Language-Action Approach to Electronic Negotiations. Systems, Signs & Actions 1(1):62–79

Schoop M (2010) Support of Complex Electronic Negotiations. In: Kilgour, D.M., Eden, C. (eds.). Advances in Group Decision and Negotiation. Springer, Dordrecht, The Netherlands, pp. 409–423

Schoop M, Booth CM (2016) Learning under the Dreaming Spires – Personalisation in Oxford Tutorials. In: Brooks L, Wainwright D, Wastell D, (eds.). UK Academy of Information Systems Conference Proceedings 2016 (UKAIS 2016), 4-13-2016 Oxford, UK, paper 46

Schoop M, Jertila A, List T (2003) Negoisst: A Negotiation Support System for Electronic Business-to-Business Negotiations in E-Commerce, Data & Knowledge Engineering 47(3):371–401

Schoop M, Köhne F, Staskiewicz D, Voeth M, Herbst, U (2008) The Antecedents of Renegotiations in Practice — An Exploratory Analysis, Group Decision and Negotiation 17(2):127–139.

Schulmeister R (2003) Lernplattformen für das virtuelle Lernen: Evaluation und Didaktik. Oldenbourg, München, Germany

Scott C (2010) The Enduring Appeal of 'Learning Styles'. Australian Journal of Education 54(1):5–17

Searle JR (1969) Speech Acts: An Essay in the Philosophy of Language. Cambridge University Press, Cambridge, USA

Sein MK, Bostrom RP (1989) Individual Differences and Conceptual Models in Training Novice Users. Human – Computer Interaction 4(3):197–229

Selim HM (2003) An Empirical Investigation of Student Acceptance of Course Websites. Computers & Education 40(4)343–360

Shaft TM, Vessey I (2006) The Role of Cognitive Fit in the Relationship between Software Comprehension and Modification. MIS Quarterly, 30(1):29–55

Shapiro C, Varian HR (1999) Information Rules: A Strategic Guide to the Network Economy, Harvard Business School Press, Boston, USA

Shea P, Bidjerano T (2010) Learning Presence. Towards a Theory of Self-Efficacy, Self-Regulation, and the Development of a Communities of Inquiry in Online and Blended Learning Environments. Computers & Education 55(4)1721–1731

Shell GR (2001) Teaching Ideas: Bargaining Styles and Negotiation: The Thomas-Kilmann Conflict Mode Instrument in Negotiation Training. Negotiation Journal 17(2):155–174

Shuell TJ (1986) Cognitive Conceptions of Learning. Review of Educational Research, 56(4):411–436

Siemens, G 2007. PLEs – I Acronym, Therefore I Exist. http://www.elearnspace.org/blog/2007/04/15/ples-i-acronym-therefore-i-exist/ Accessed 27 April 2015

Simon HA (1996) The Sciences of the Artificial. 3. ed., MIT Press, Cambridge, USA

Skinner BF (1958) Teaching Machines: From the Experimental Study of Learning Come Devices Which Arrange Optimal Conditions for Self-Instruction. Science, 128(3330):969–977

Steiner CM, Albert D, Nussbaumer A (2009) Supporting Self-Regulated Personalised Learning through Competence-Based Knowledge Space Theory. Policy Futures in Education, 7(6):645

Strayer JF (2012) How Learning in an Inverted Classroom Influences Cooperation, Innovation and Task Orientation. Learning Environments Research 15(2):171–193

Ströbel M, Weinhardt C (2003) The Montreal Taxonomy for Electronic Negotiations, Group Decision and Negotiation (12), pp. 143–164

Sun J, Wang Y (2014) Tool Choice for E-Learning: Task-Technology Fit
through Media Synchronicity. Information Systems Education Journal,
12(4):17-28

Sun PC, Tsai RJ, Finger G, Chen YY, Yeh D (2008) What Drives a Successful E-Learning? An Empirical Investigation of the Critical Factors
Influencing Student Satisfaction. Computers & Education 50(4)1183–
1202

Sung YP (2009) An Analysis of the Technology Acceptance Model in Understanding University Students' Behavioral Intention to Use E-Learning. Journal of Educational Technology & Society 12(3):150–162

Swan M (2012) Sensor Mania! The Internet of Things, Wearable Computing, Objective Metrics, and the Quantified Self 2.0. Journal of Sensor
and Actuator Networks, 1(3):217–253

Sweller J (1988) Cognitive Load During Problem Solving: Effects on Learning. Cognitive Science 12(2):257–285

Sweller J (1994) Cognitive Load Theory, Learning Difficulty, and Instructional Design. Learning and Instruction 4(4):295–312

Taggart W, Robey D, Taggart B (1982) Decision Styles Education: An Innovative Approach, Journal of Management Education 7(2):17–24

Tapscott D, Williams AD (2010) Innovating the 21st-Century University: It's
Time! EDUCAUSE Review, 45(1):16–29

Tennyson RD (1992) An Educational Learning Theory for Instructional Design. Educational Technology, 32(1):36–41

Thayer HS (2012) Pragmatism: The Classic Writings; Charles Sanders
Peirce, William James, Clarence Irving Lewis, John Dewey, George
Herbert Mead. In: Thayer HS (ed.) Hackett, Indianapolis, USA

Thompson L (1990) The Influence of Experience on Negotiation Performance. Journal of Experimental Social Psychology 26:528–544

Tsai CW, Shen PD, Fan YT (2013) Research Trends in Self-Regulated
Learning Research in Online Learning Environments: A Review of
Studies Published in Selected Journals from 2003 to 2012. British Jour-
nal of Educational Technology, 44(5):E107-E110

U.S. Department of Education (2010) Transforming American Education: Learning Powered by Technology: National Educational Technology Plan 2010. Available at: http://www.ed.gov/sites/de-
fault/files/NETP-2010-final-report.pdf Accessed 12-3-2016

van Merrienboer JJG, Sweller J (2010) Cognitive Load Theory in Health Professional Education: Design Principles and Strategies. Medical Education, 44(1):85–93

Venable JR, Pries-Heje J, Baskerville RL (2016) FEDS: A Framework for Evaluation in Design Science Research. European Journal of Information Systems, 25(1):77–89

Venkatesh V, Bala H (2008) Technology Acceptance Model 3 and a Research Agenda on Interventions. Decision Sciences, 39(2):273–315

Venkatesh V, Brown SA, Bala H (2013) Bridging the Qualitative-Quantitative Divide: Guidelines for Conducting Mixed Methods Research in Information Systems. MIS Quarterly, 37(1):21–54

Vermunt JD (1996) Metacognitive, Cognitive and Affective Aspects of Learning Styles and Strategies: A Phenomenographic Analysis, Higher Education 31(1):25–50

Vessey I (1991) Cognitive Fit: A Theory-Based Analysis of the Graphs Versus Tables Literature. Decision Sciences, 22(2):219–240

Vessey I Galletta, D (1991) Cognitive Fit: An Empirical Study of Information Acquisition, Information Systems Research 2(1):63–84

Vessey I, Weber R (1986) Structured Tools and Conditional Logic: An Empirical Investigation, Communications of the ACM 29(1):48–57

Vetschera R, Kersten G, Köszegi S (2006) User Assessment of Internet-Based Negotiation Support Systems: An Exploratory Study. Journal of Organizational Computing and Electronic Commerce 16(2):123–148

Walther JB, Parks MR (2011) Cues Filtered Out, Cues Filtered In. In: Knapp ML, Daly, JA (eds.), Handbook of Interpersonal Communication. 4th ed., pp. 529–63. Sage, Los Angeles, USA

Wang F, Hannafin MJ (2005) Design-Based Research and Technology-Enhanced Learning Environments. Educational Technology Research and Development, 53(4):5–23

Weale S (2017) Teachers Must Ditch 'Neuromyth' of Learning Styles, Say Scientists. Available at: https://www.theguardian.com/education/2017/mar/13/teachers-neuromyth-learning-styles-scientists-neuroscience-education Accessed 3-23-2017

Woolfolk A (2014) Pädagogische Psychologie. 12th ed. Pearson, Hallbergmoos, Germany

Zimmerman BJ (1989) A Social Cognitive View of Self-Regulated Academic Learning. Journal of Educational Psychology, 81(3):329–339

Zimmerman BJ (2002) Becoming a Self-Regulated Learner: An Overview. Theory into Practice, 41(2):64–70

Printed in the United States
By Bookmasters